ACOUSTIC MASTERS *for*

MW00812245

PAUL SIMON

Kodachrome ® is a registered trademark for colour film

WISE PUBLICATIONS
part of The Music Sales Group
London / New York / Paris / Sydney / Copenhagen / Berlin / Madrid / Tokyo

50 WAYS TO LEAVE YOUR LOVER

WORDS & MUSIC BY PAUL SIMON

free._____ Ooh slip out the back,_____ Jack. Make a new

plan,_____ Stan. You don't need to be coy,_____ Roy. You just lis-ten to me._____

Hop on the bus,_____ Gus. You don't need to dis-cuss_____ much_____ just drop off the

key,_____ Lee and get your-self_____ free._____

Solo drums to fade

DUNCAN

WORDS & MUSIC BY PAUL SIMON

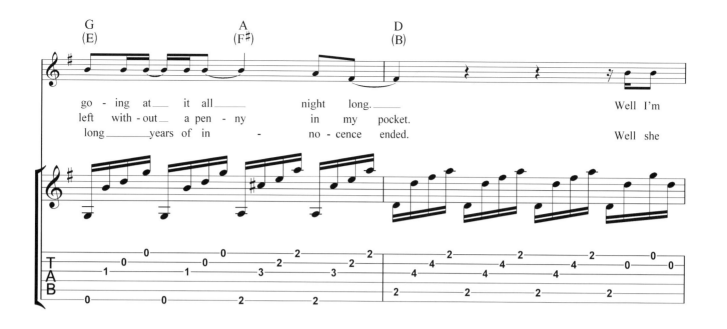

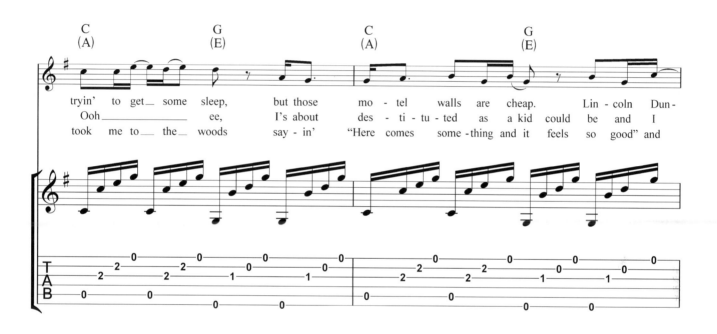

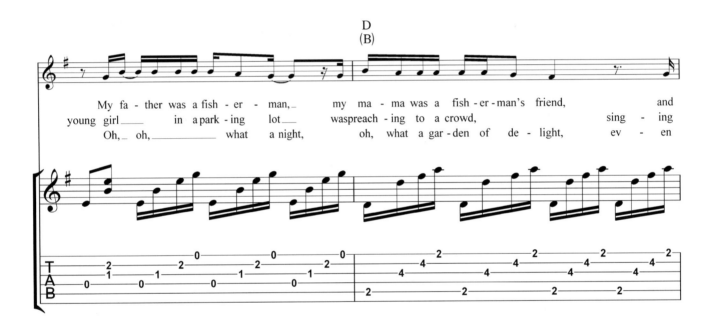

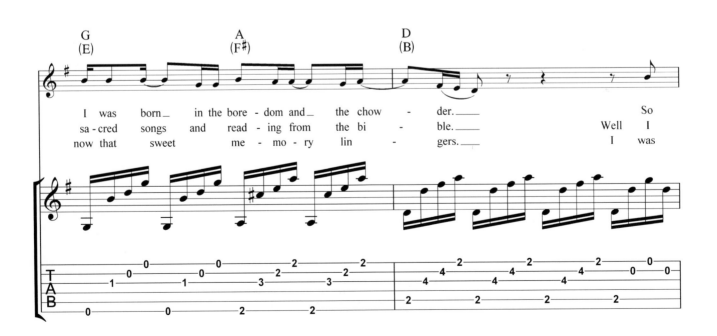

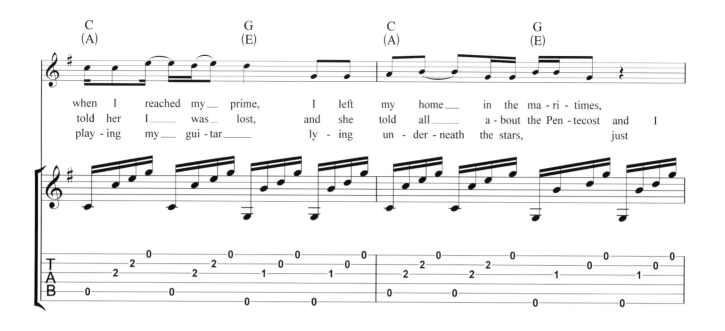

when I reached my prime, I left my home in the ma - ri - times,
told her I was lost, and she told all a - bout the Pen - tecost and I
play - ing my gui - tar ly - ing un - der - neath the stars, just

head - ed down the turn - pike for New Eng - land; sweet New Eng -
seen that girl as the road to my sur - vi - val,
thank - ing the Lord for my fin - gers, for my fin -

Bridge

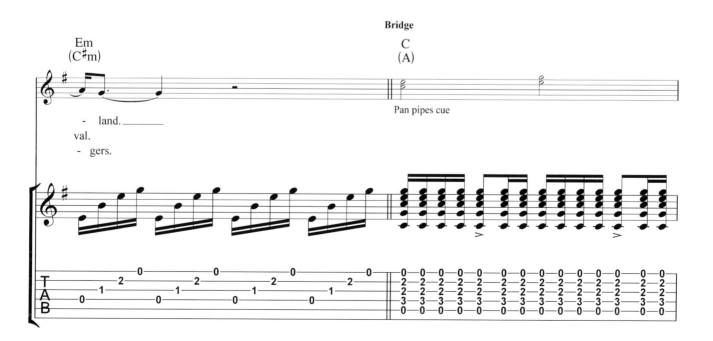

- land.
val.
- gers.

Pan pipes cue

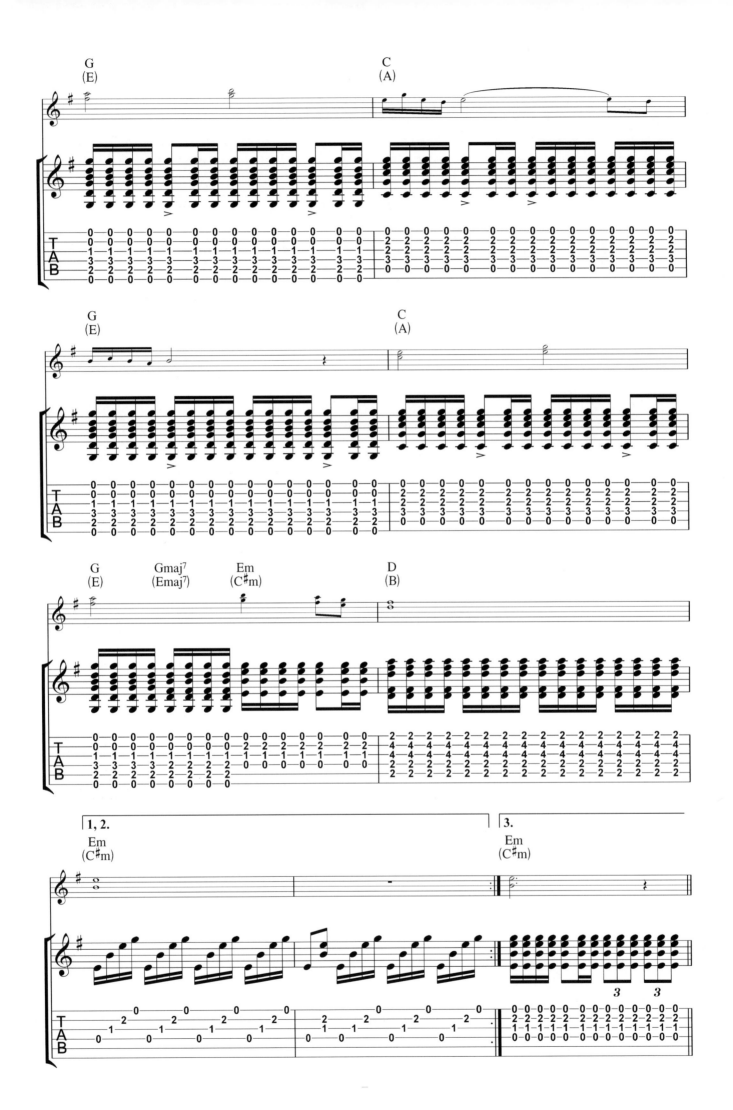

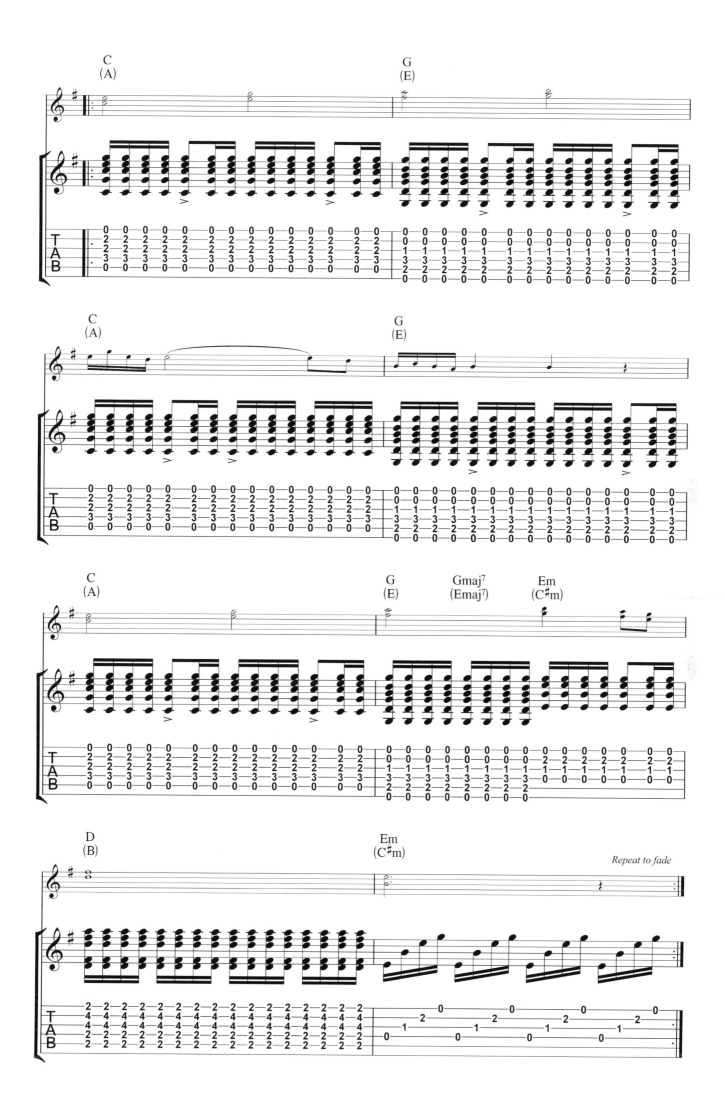

EVERYTHING PUT TOGETHER FALLS APART

WORDS & MUSIC BY PAUL SIMON

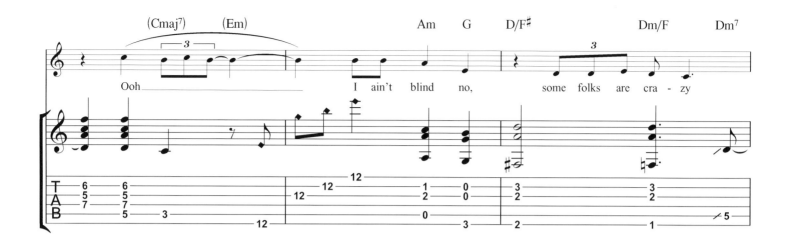

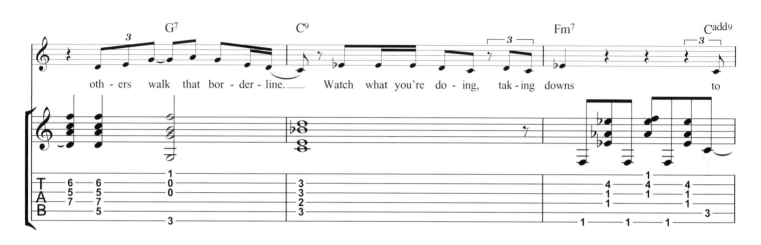

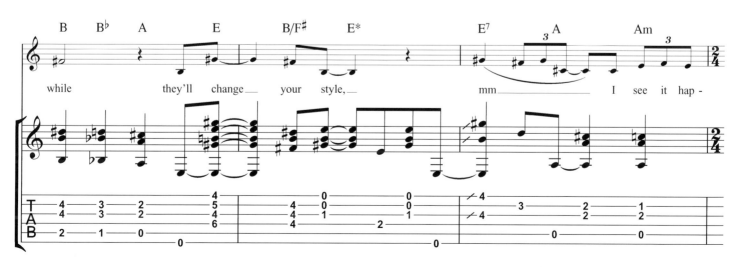

HEARTS AND BONES

WORDS & MUSIC BY PAUL SIMON

One and one half wan - der - ing Jews, _____ free to wan-

- der wher - ev - er_____ they choose, _____ are trav-

- 'ling to - ge - ther in the San - gre de Cris - to, in the

Blood of___ Christ moun - tains in New Mex - i - co.___

bones.

2. Think - ing

back_____ to the sea - son be - fore,   look - ing back_____

3. (⅗) One   and   one half wan - der - ing Jews_____   re -

_____ through   the   cracks   in   the   door.

turn_____   to   their   na - ta - ral   coasts,_____   Two   peo - ple

to   re -

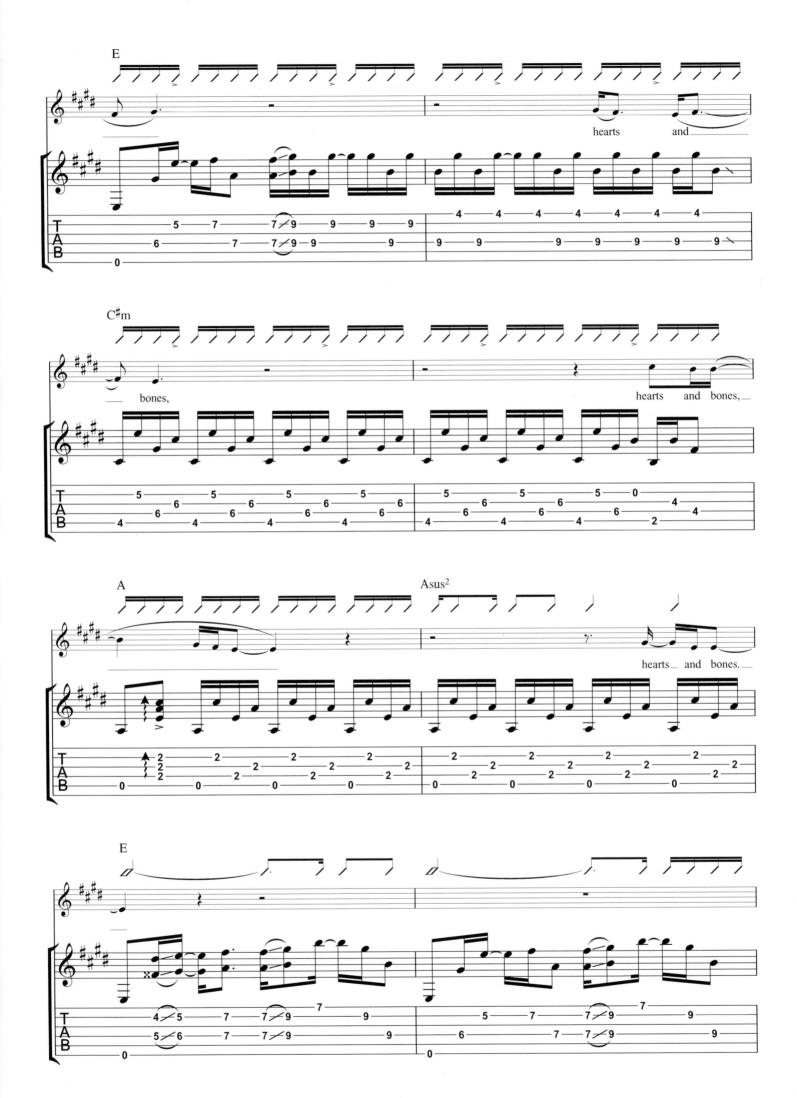

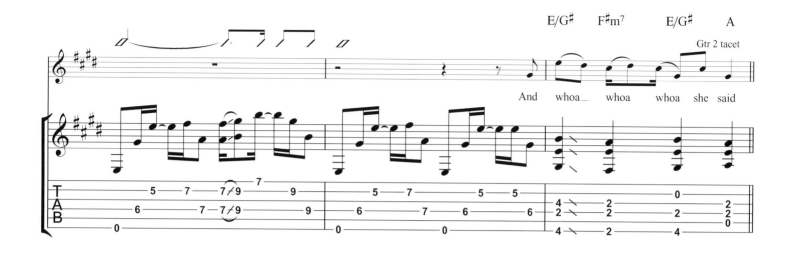

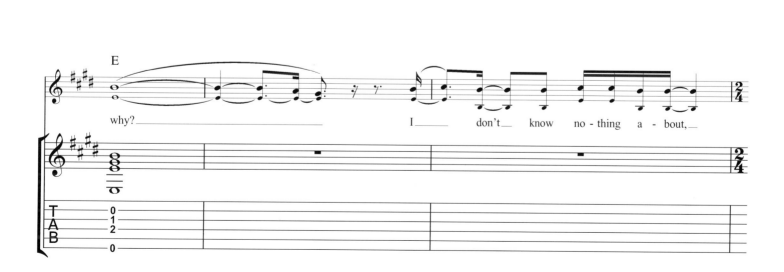

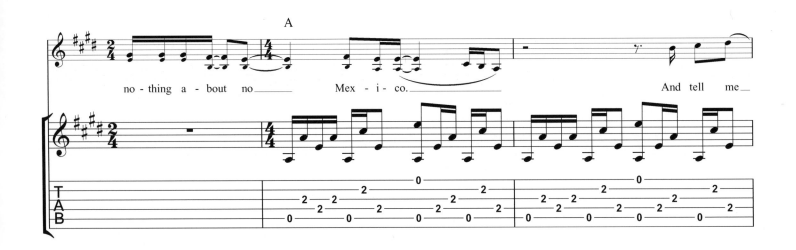

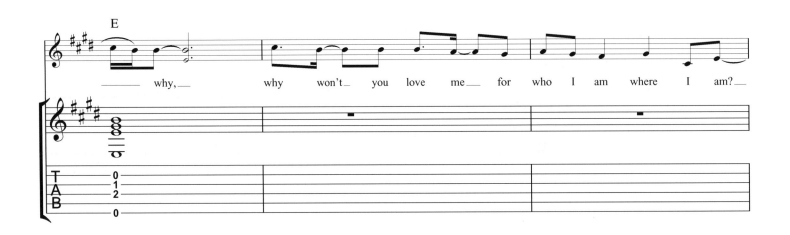

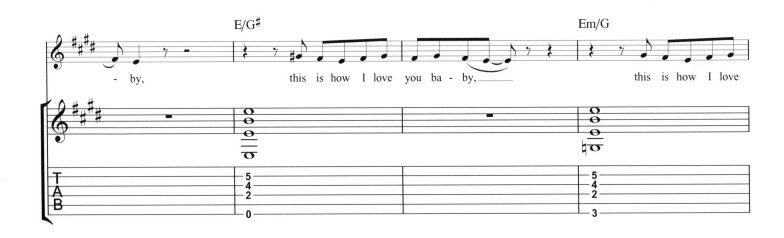

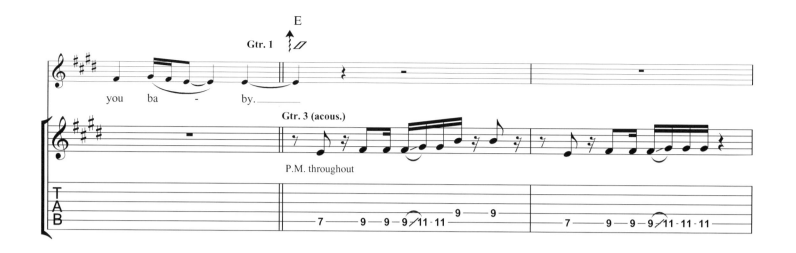

you ba - by.___

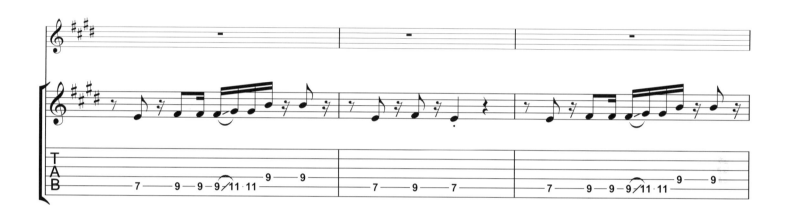

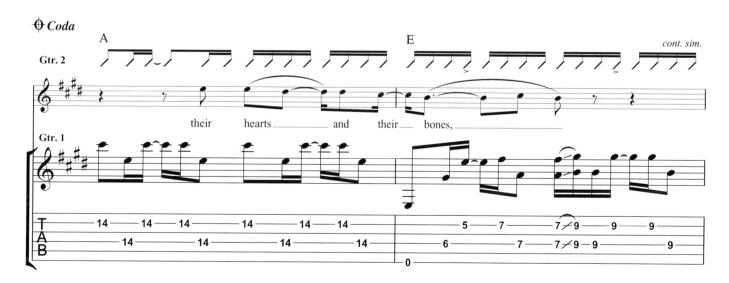

their   hearts___ and   their___ bones,___

HOW THE HEART APPROACHES
WHAT IT YEARNS

WORDS & MUSIC BY PAUL SIMON

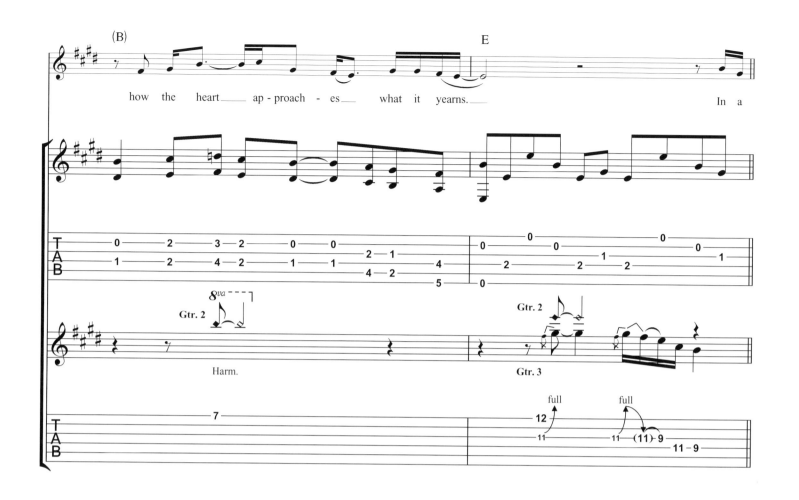

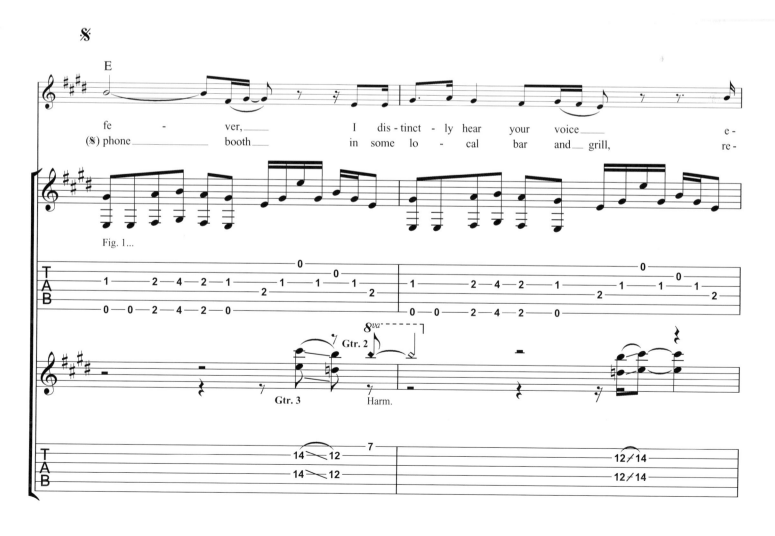

31

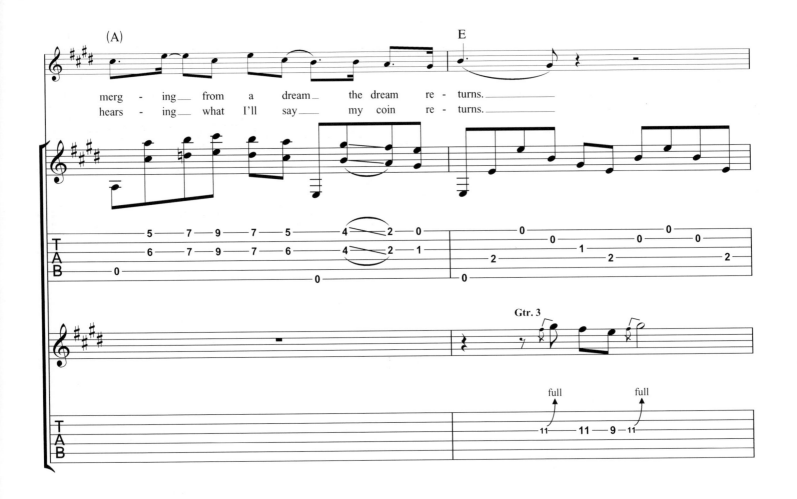

merg - ing___ from a dream___ the dream re - turns.___
hears - ing___ what I'll say___ my coin re - turns.___

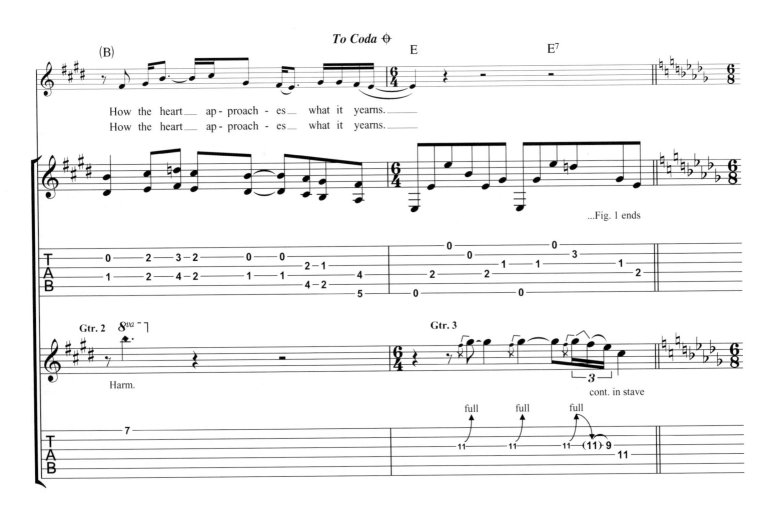

How the heart___ ap - proach - es___ what it yearns.___
How the heart___ ap - proach - es___ what it yearns.___

...Fig. 1 ends

Gtr. 2 8va

Harm.

Gtr. 3

cont. in stave

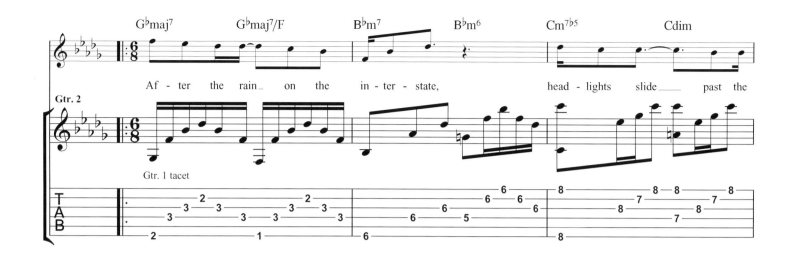

Af - ter the rain on the in - ter - state, head - lights slide past the

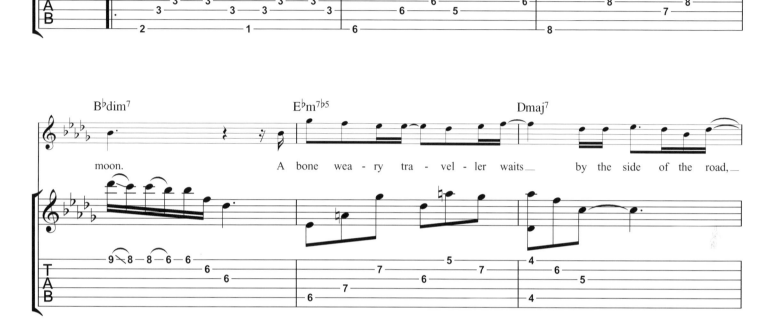

moon. A bone wea - ry tra - vel - er waits by the side of the road,

where's he go - ing?

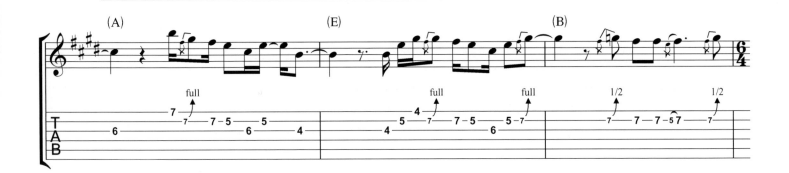

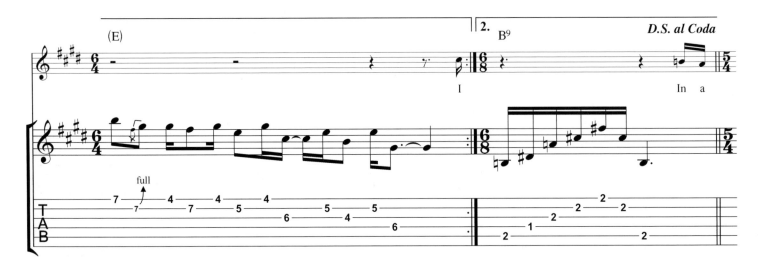

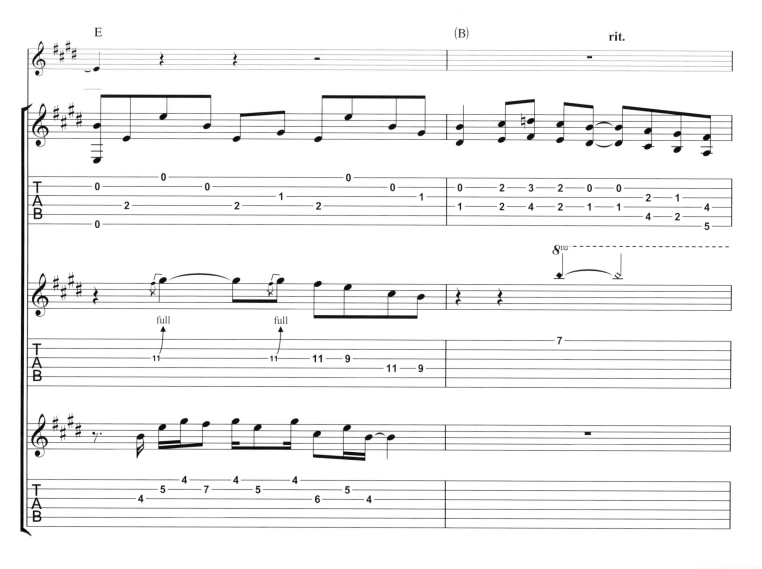

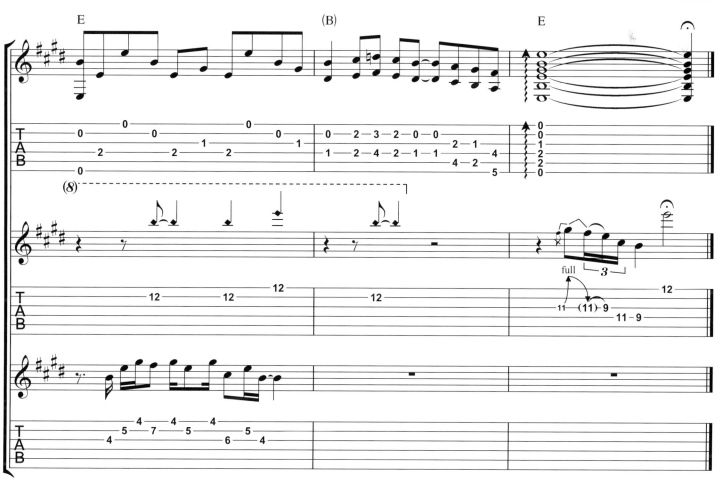

KODACHROME®

WORDS & MUSIC BY PAUL SIMON

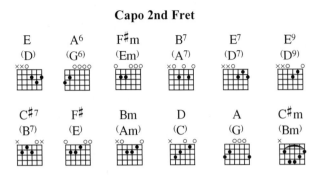

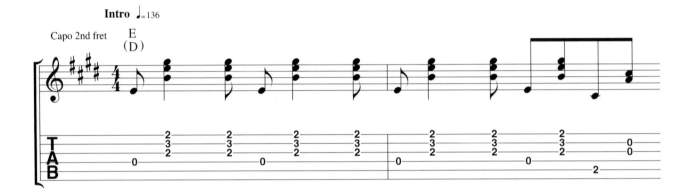

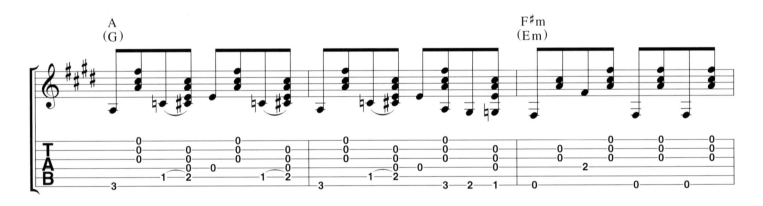

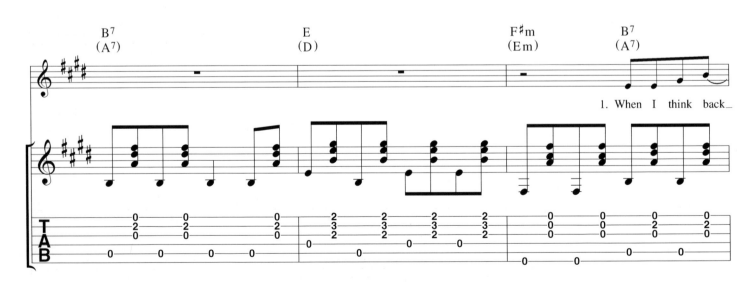

1. When I think back

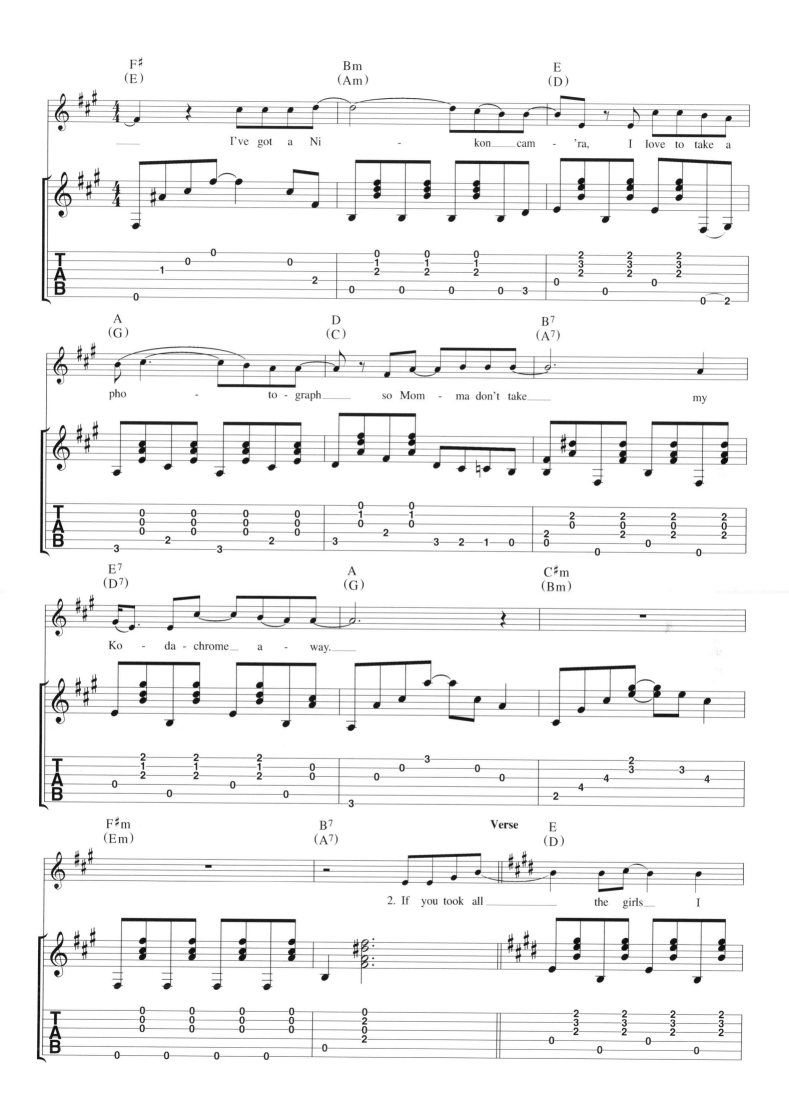

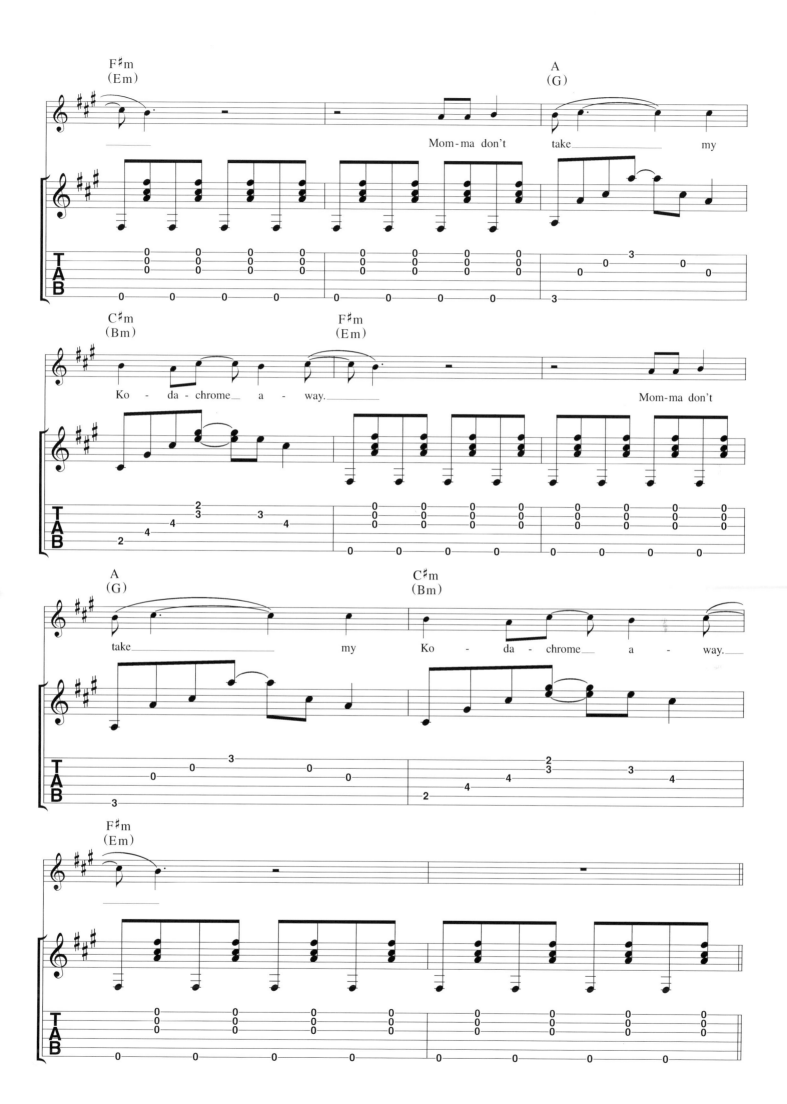

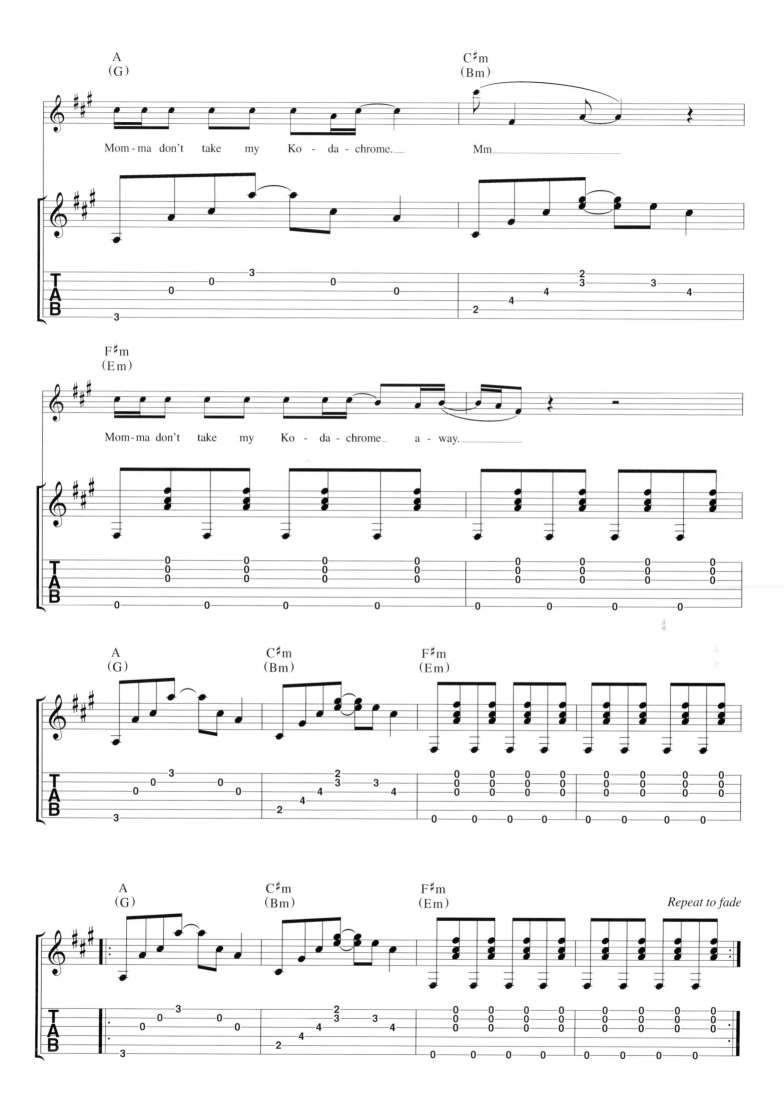

THE LATE GREAT JOHNNY ACE

WORDS & MUSIC BY PAUL SIMON
CODA BY PHILIP GLASS

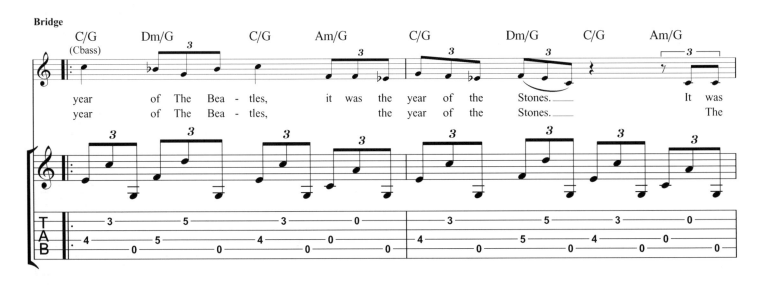

Bridge

year   of The Bea - tles,   it   was   the   year   of   the   Stones.____   It   was
year   of The Bea - tles,   the   year   of   the   Stones.____   The

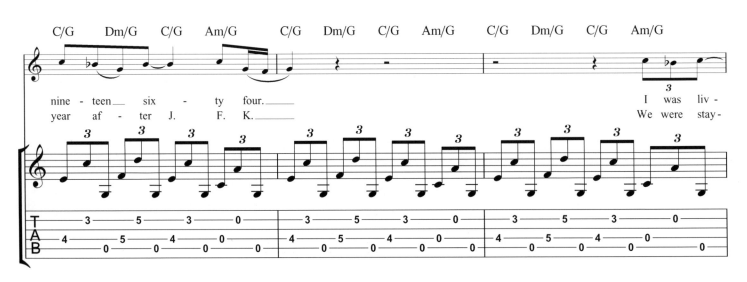

nine - teen___ six - ty four.____   I was liv -
year af - ter J.   F.   K.____   We were stay -

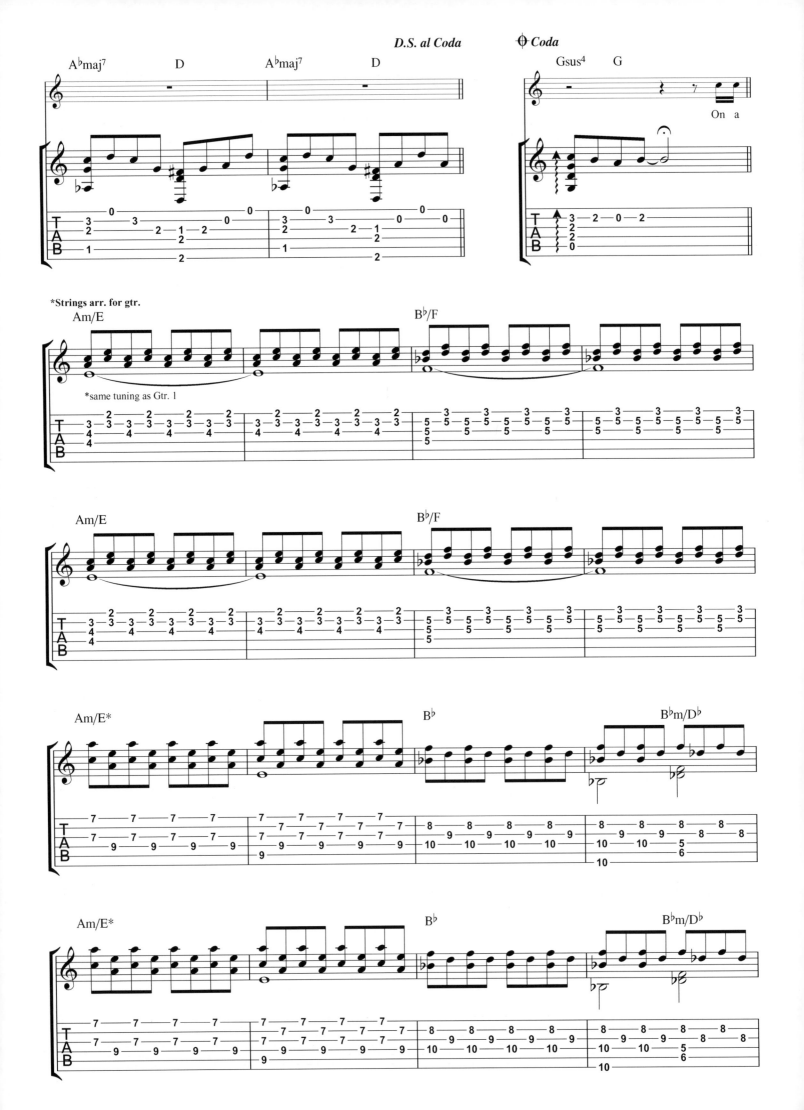

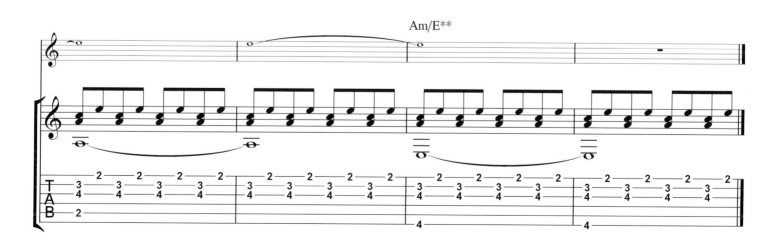

ARMISTICE DAY

WORDS & MUSIC BY PAUL SIMON

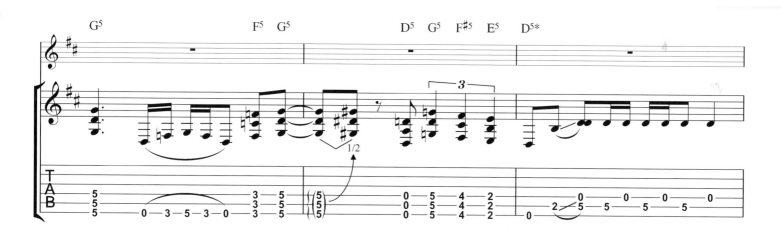

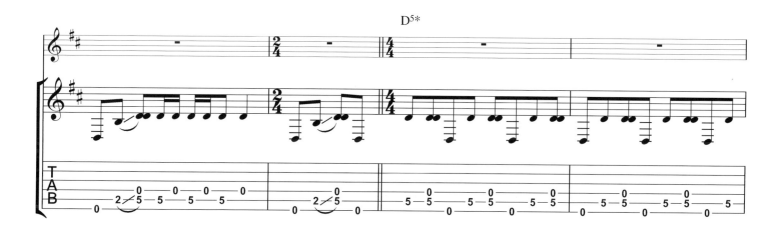

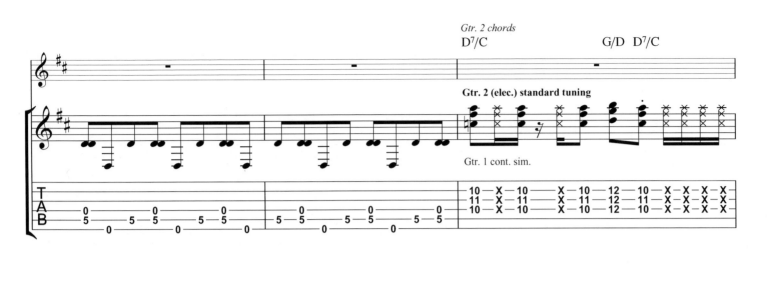

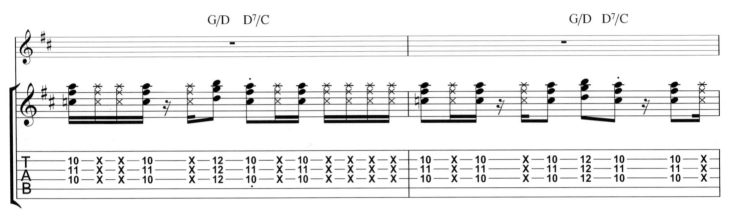

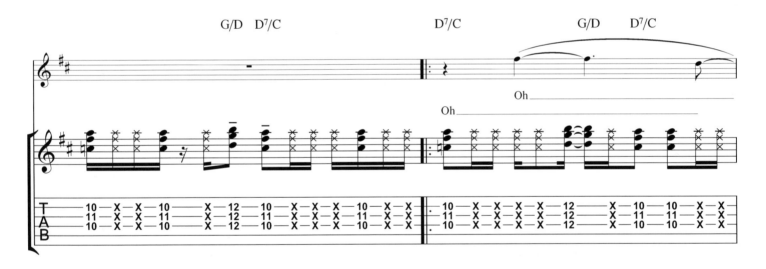

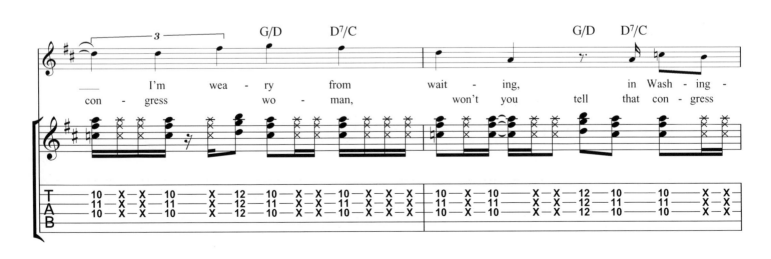

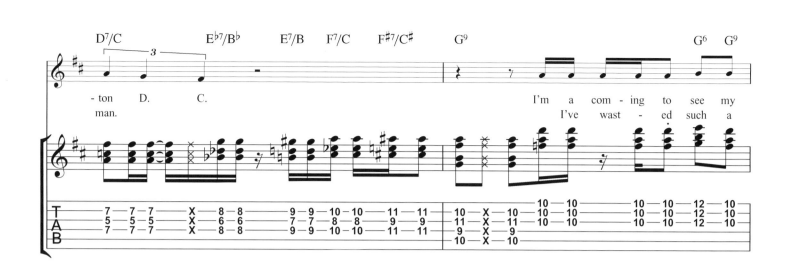
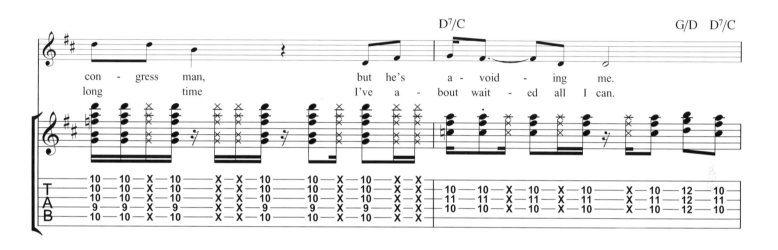
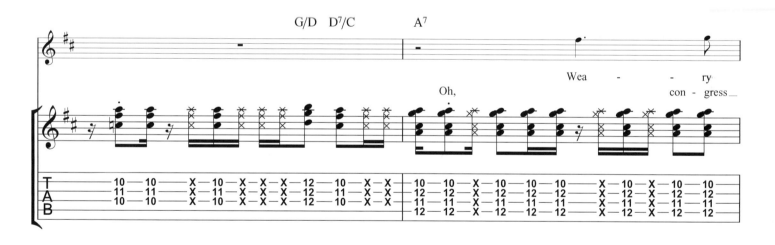
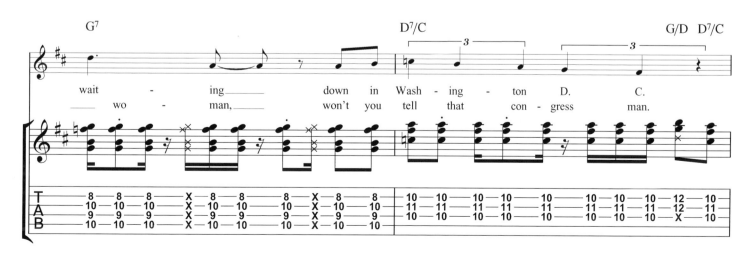

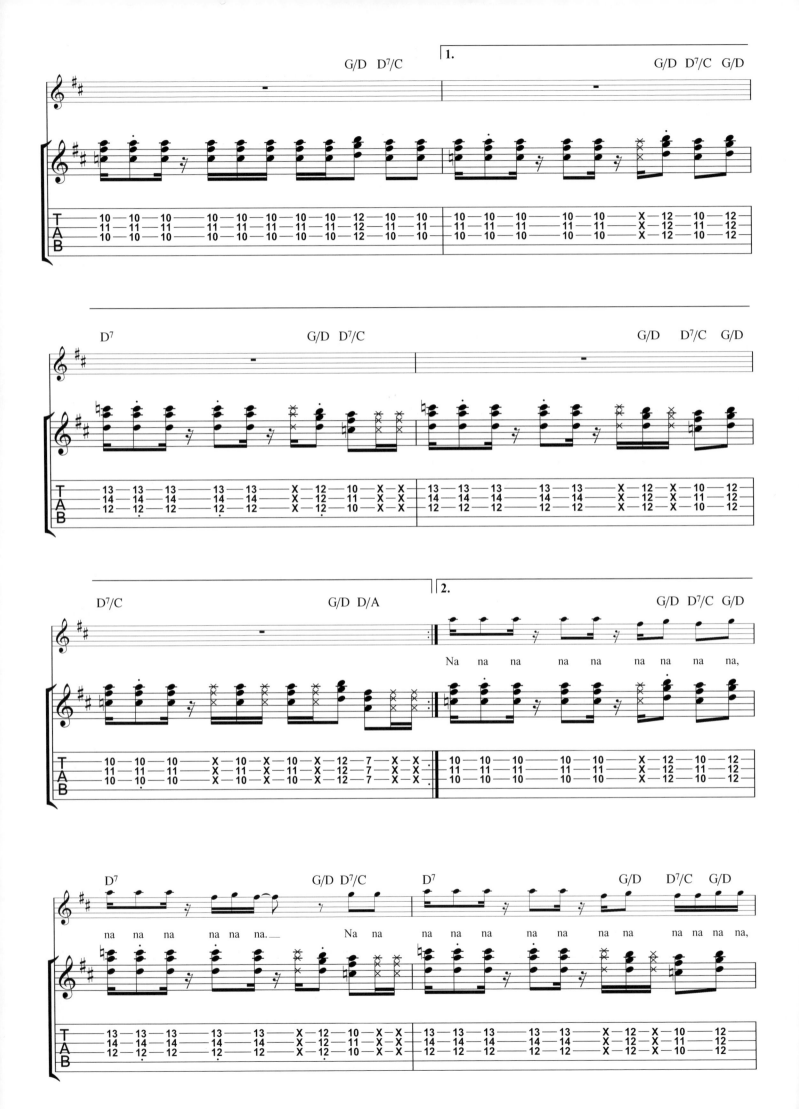

LEARN HOW TO FALL

WORDS & MUSIC BY PAUL SIMON

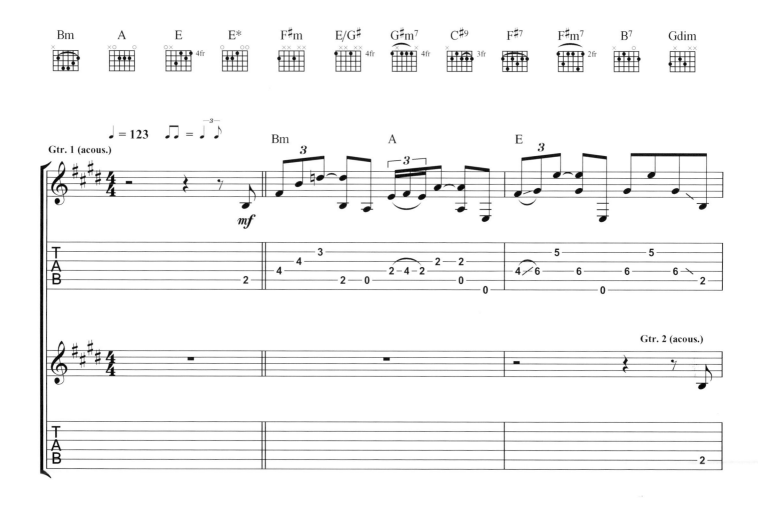

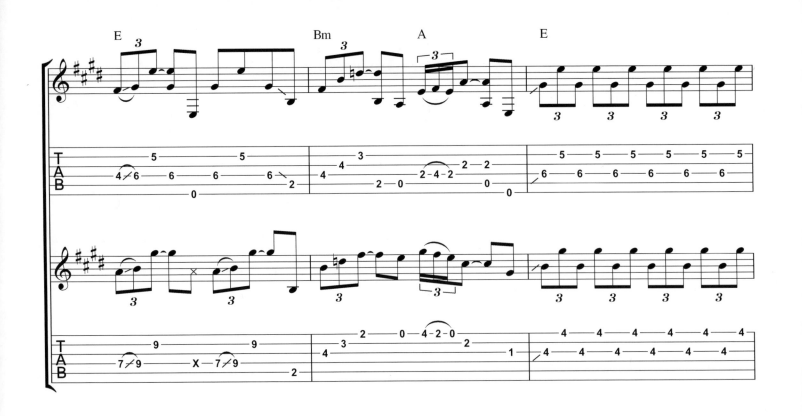

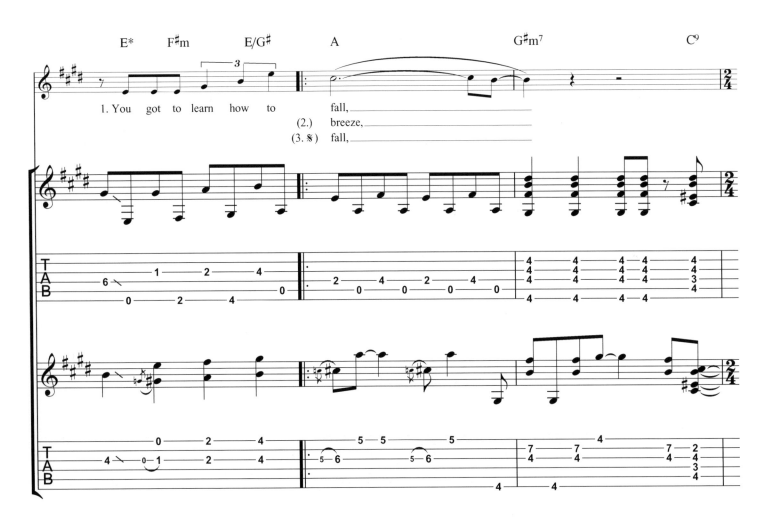

1. You got to learn how to fall,
(2.) breeze,
(3. %) fall,

learn   how   to   fall.
drift   in   the   breeze.
learn   how   to   fall.

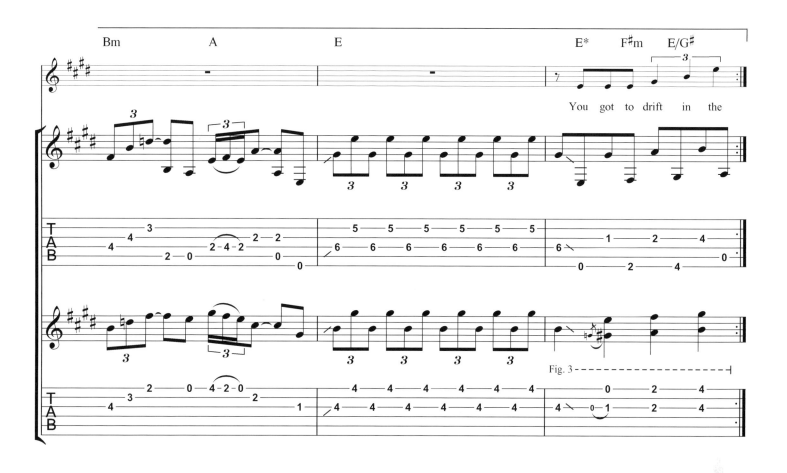

2. Bridge

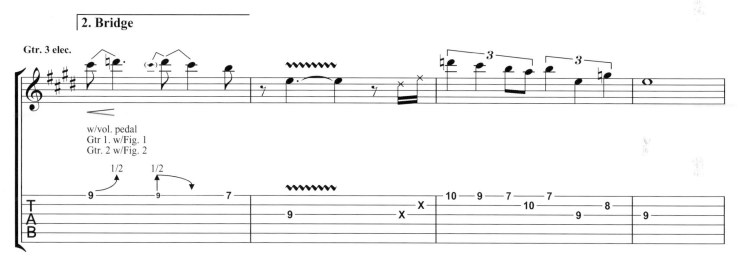

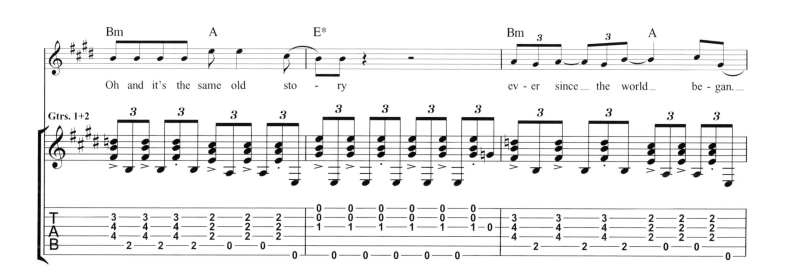

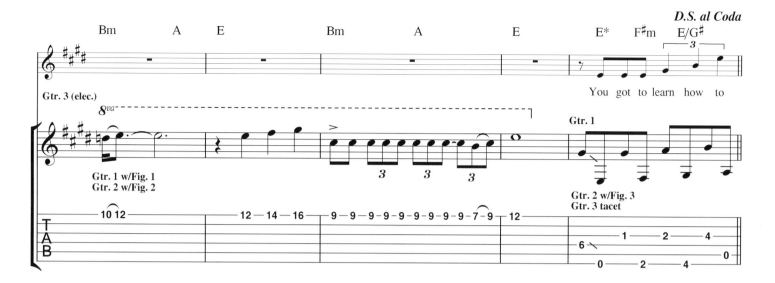

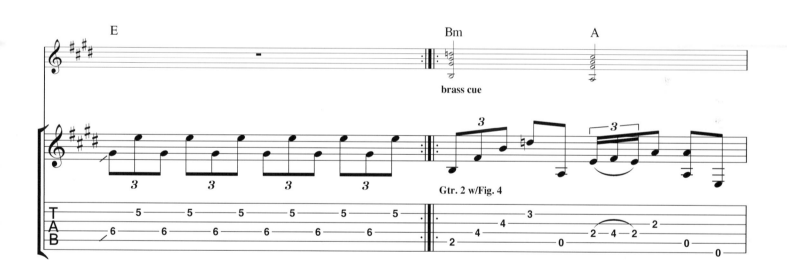

LOVE

WORDS & MUSIC BY PAUL SIMON

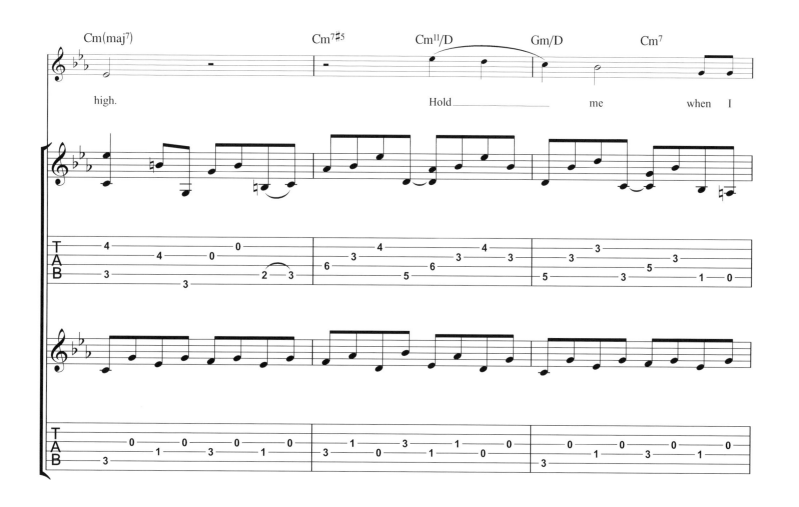

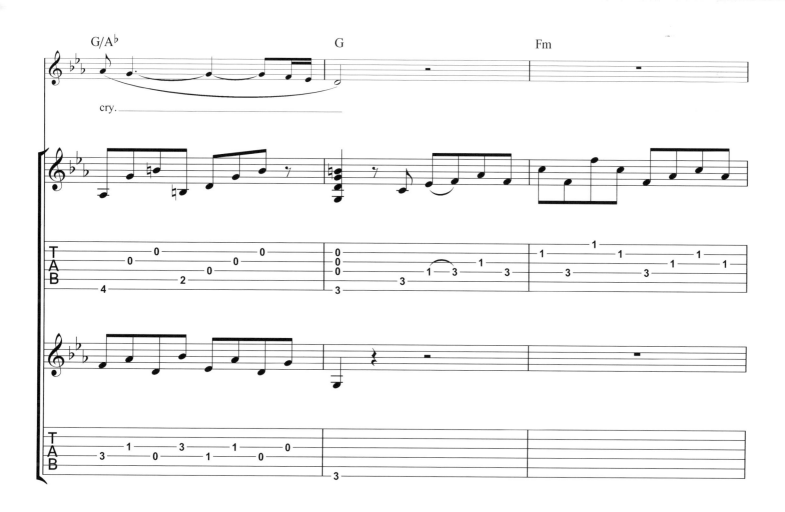

Like plants the me - di - cine is ev - 'ry - where.____

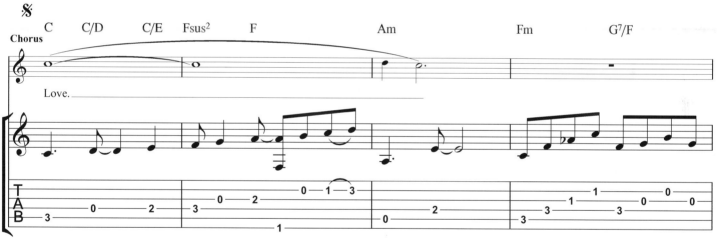

Love.____

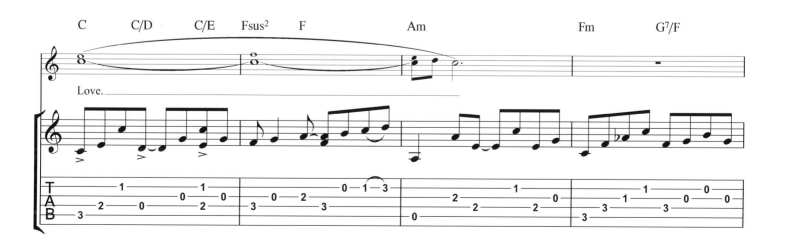

Love.____

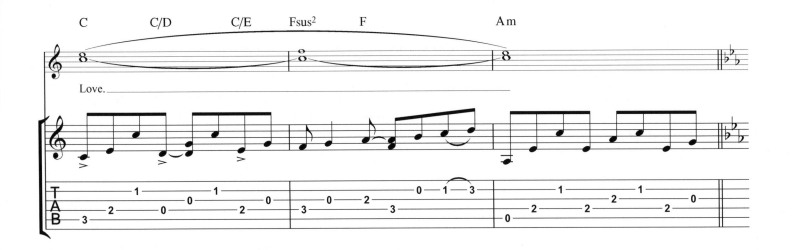

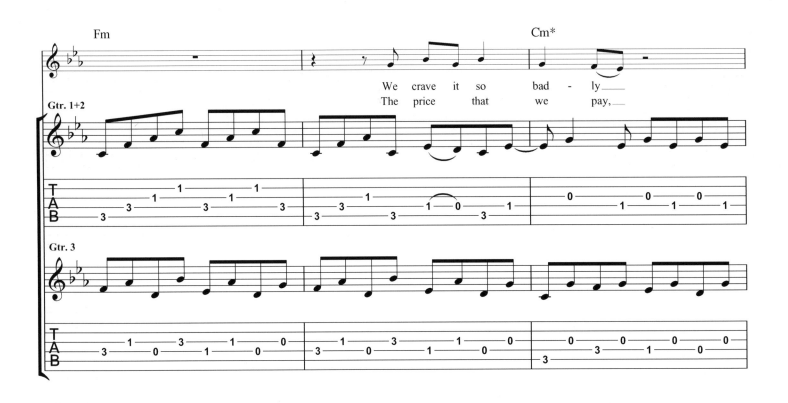

72

can - dy.

Cm   B♭m/F

Bridge
A♭   A♭*   A♭6   D♭/F*   E♭/G

We think it's ea - sy,   some - times it's ea - sy,   but it's not ea - sy,

Gtrs. 1+2

Gtr. 3

Gtr. 4

Gtr. 4 (elec. 12 str.)

73

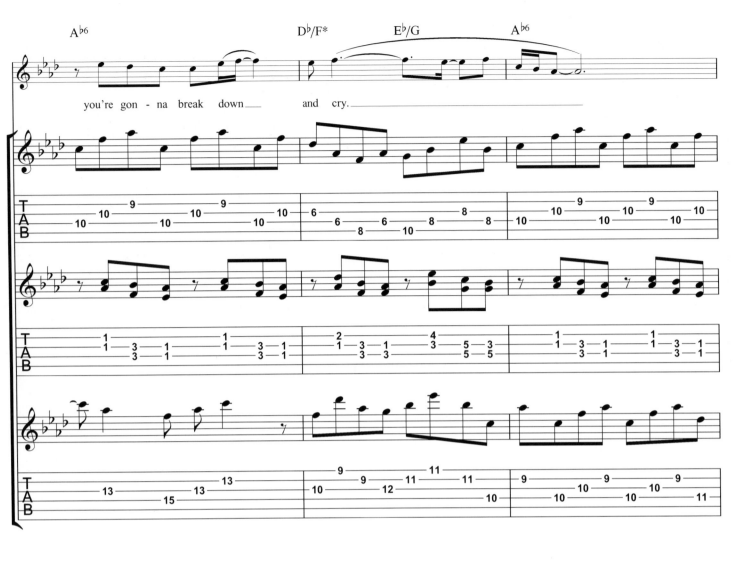

you're gon - na break down___ and cry.___

We're not im - por - tant,___ we should be grate - ful, and if you're won - der - ing why.___

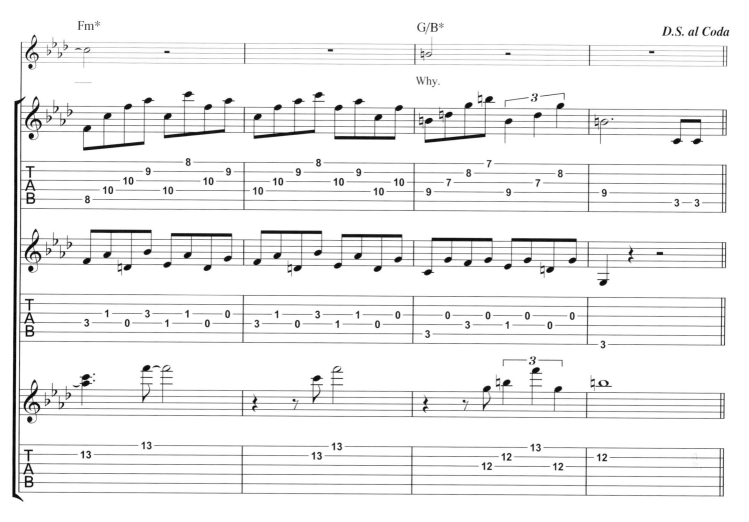

the cho - sen peo - ples,   the burn -

- ing tem - ples,   the weep - ing   ca - the - drals.

77

ME AND JULIO DOWN BY THE SCHOOLYARD

WORDS & MUSIC BY PAUL SIMON

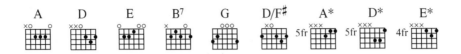

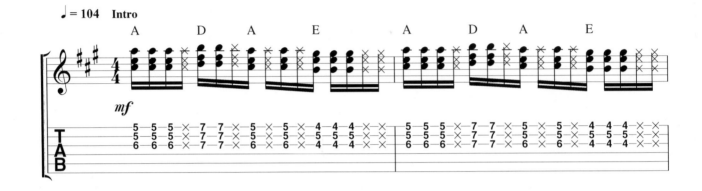

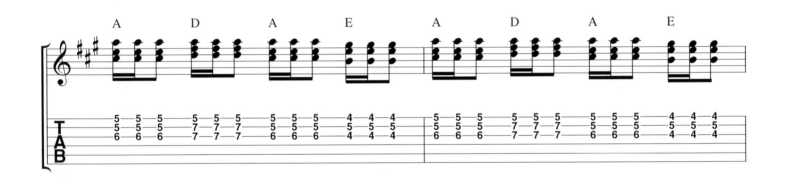

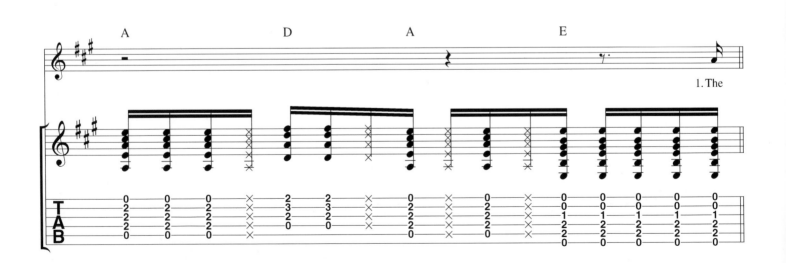

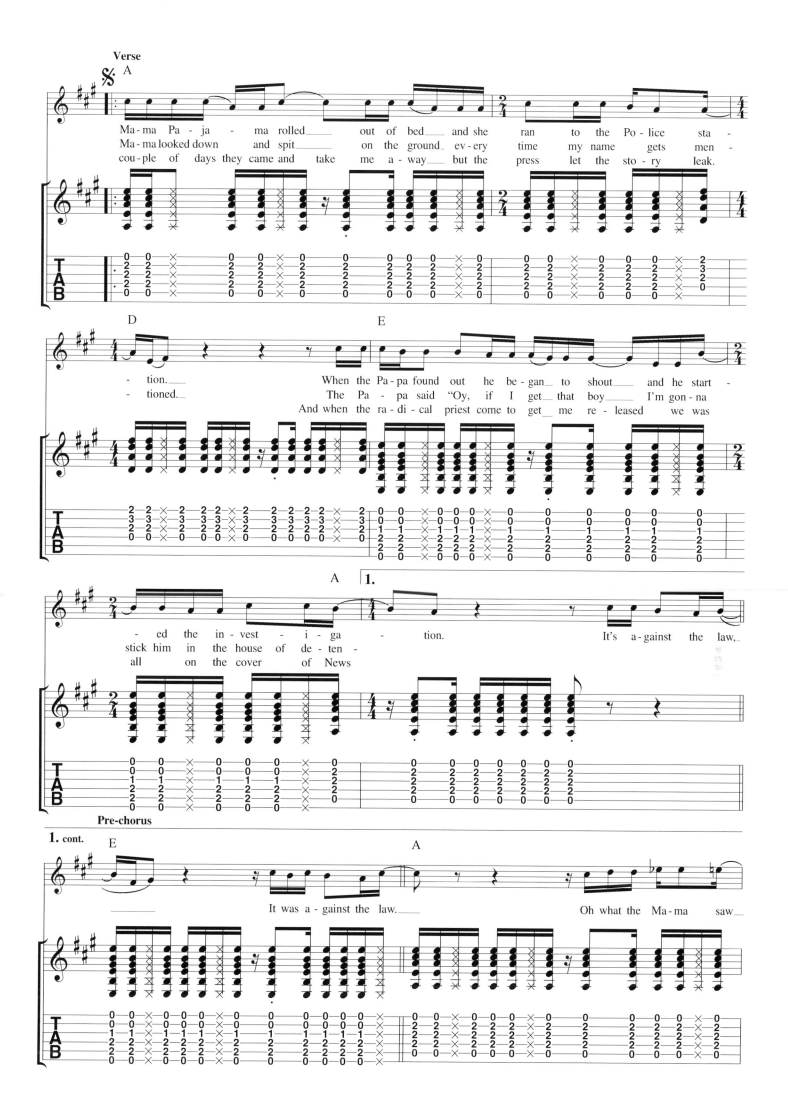

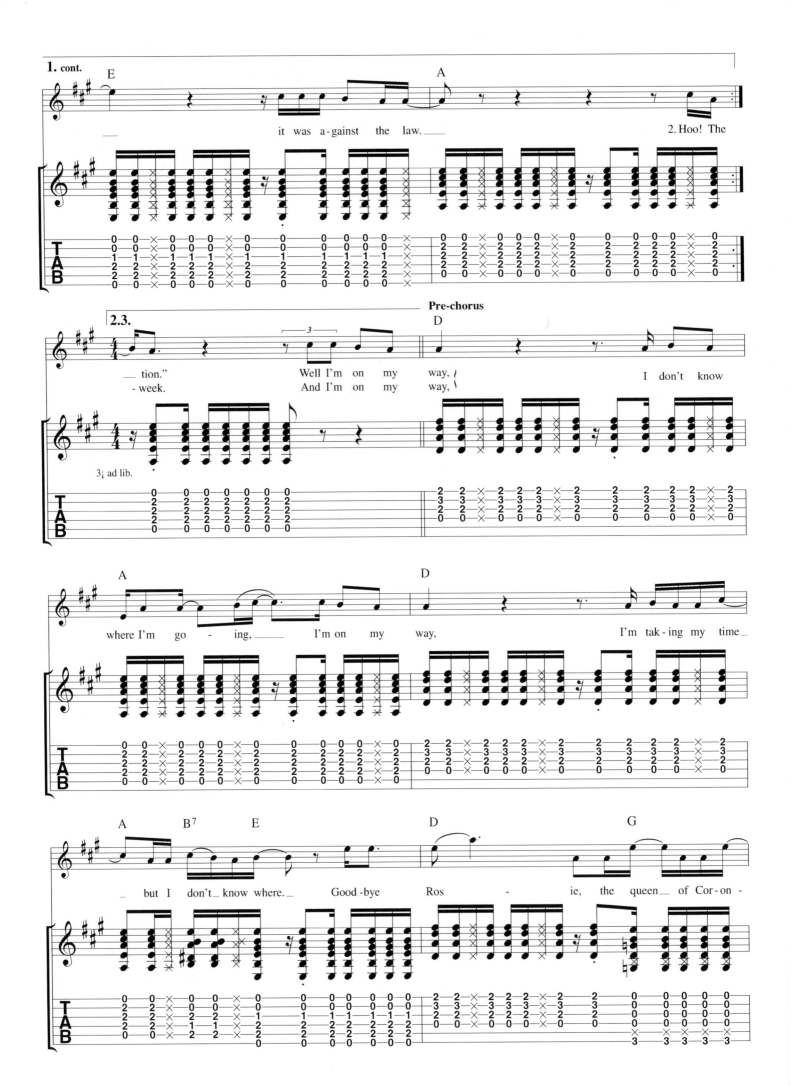

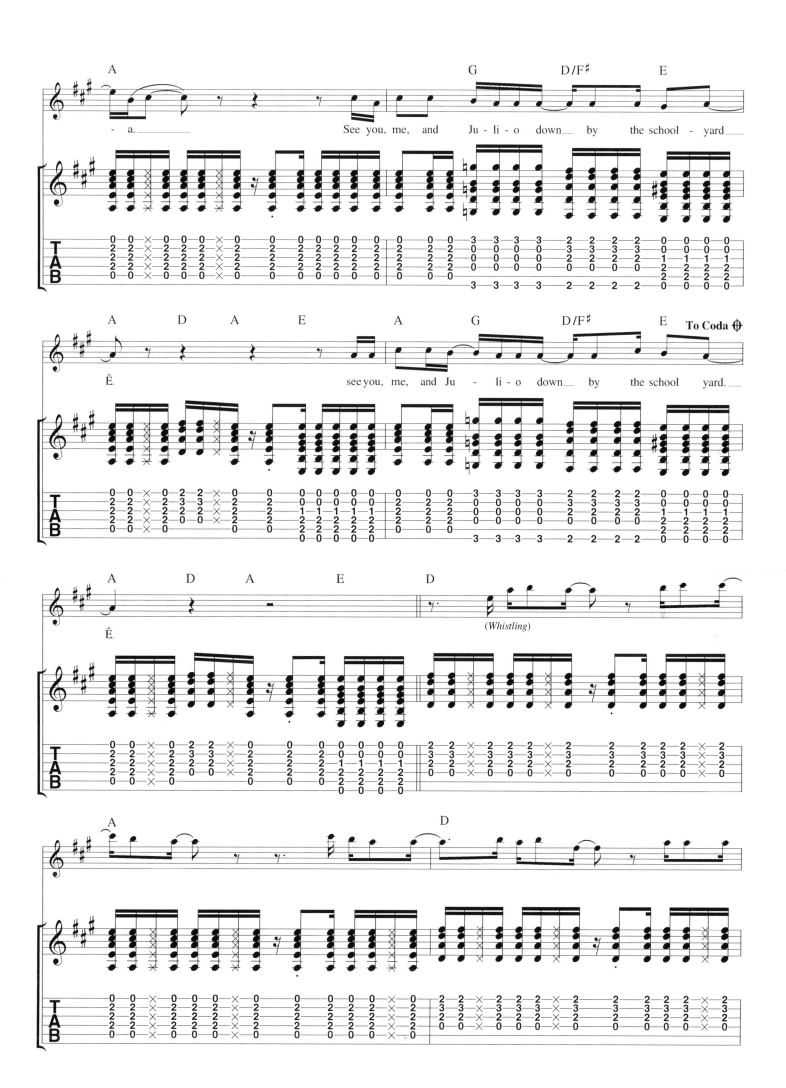

See you, me, and Ju - li - o down by the school - yard

see you, me, and Ju - li - o down by the school yard.

(Whistling)

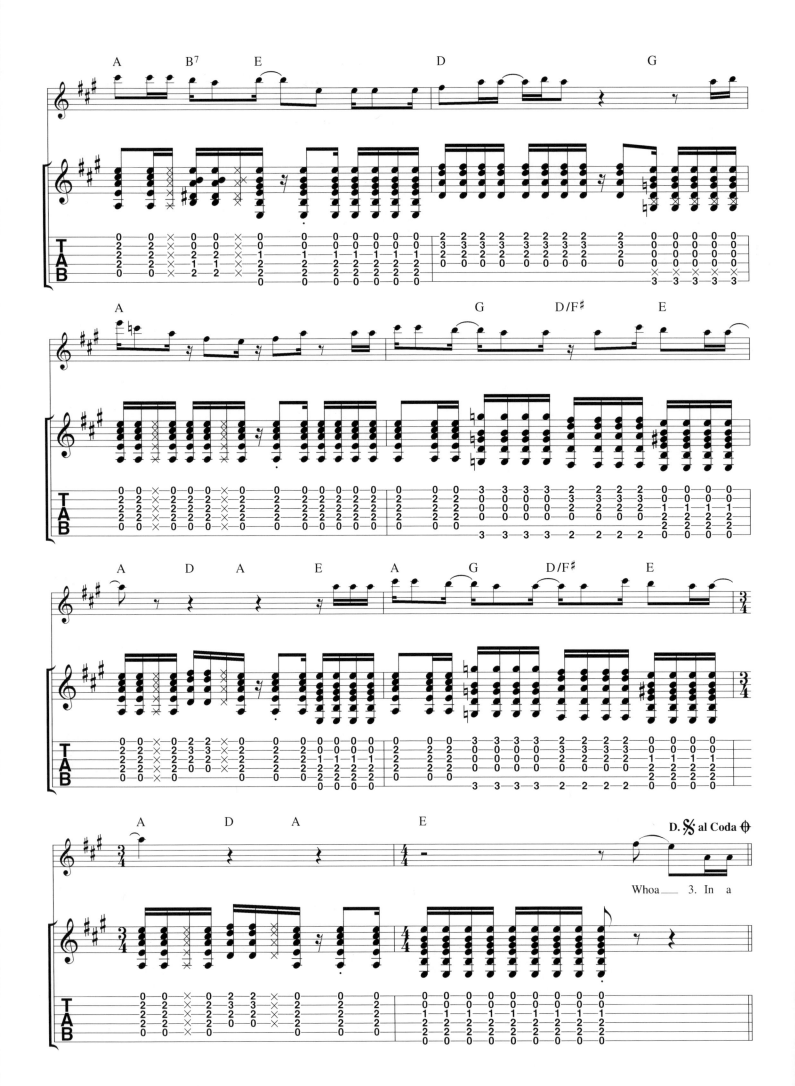

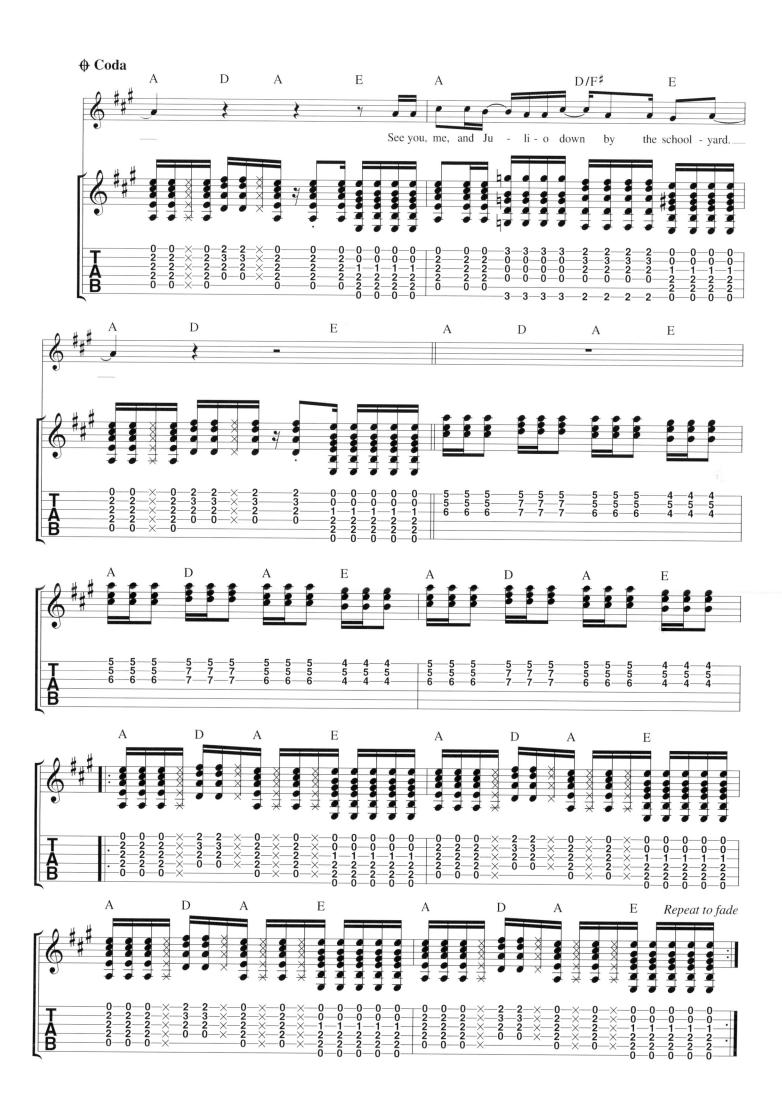

PAPA HOBO

WORDS & MUSIC BY PAUL SIMON

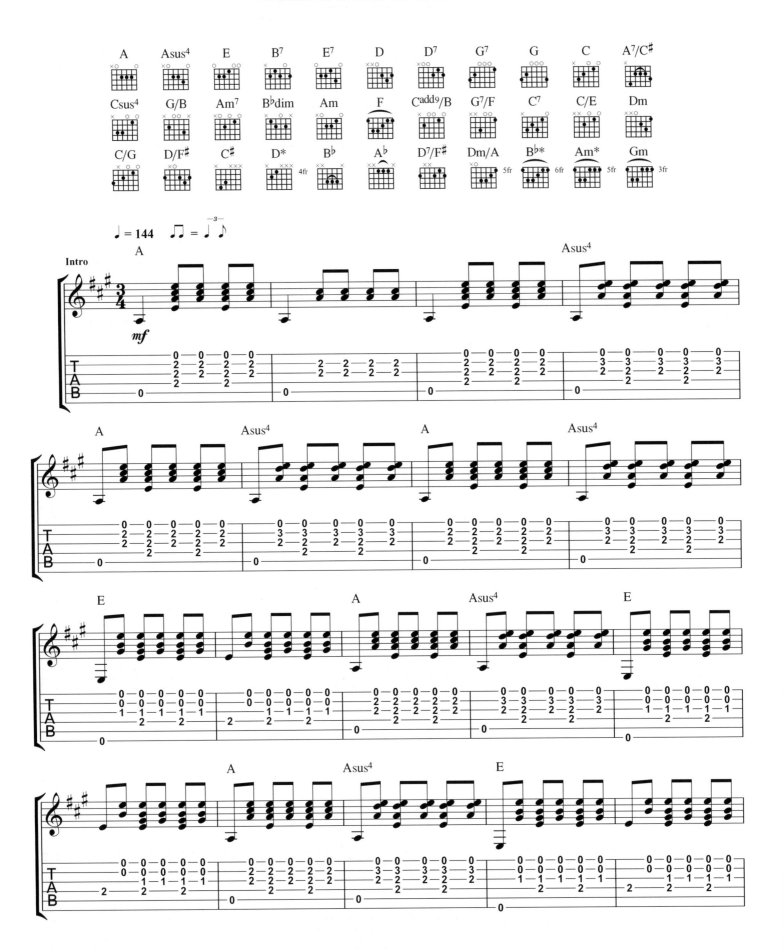

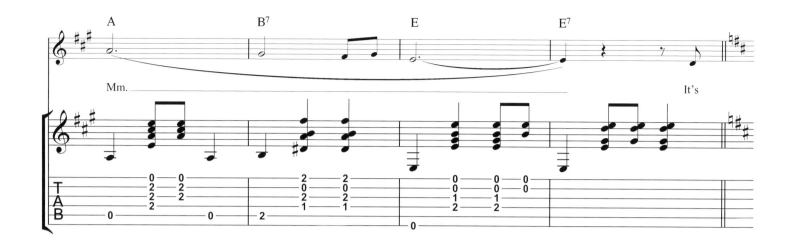

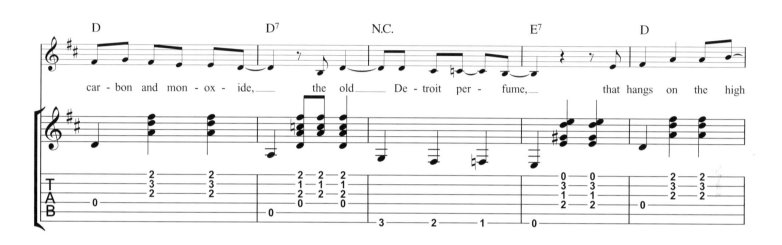

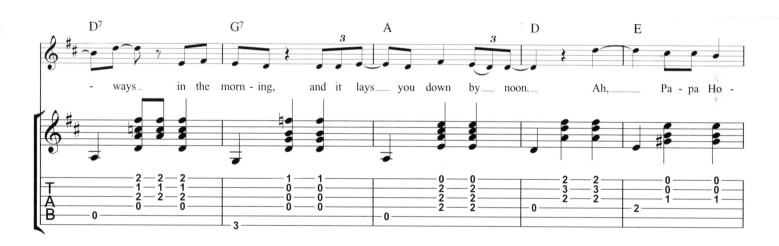

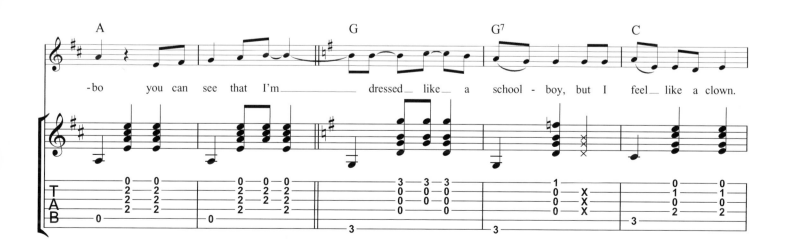

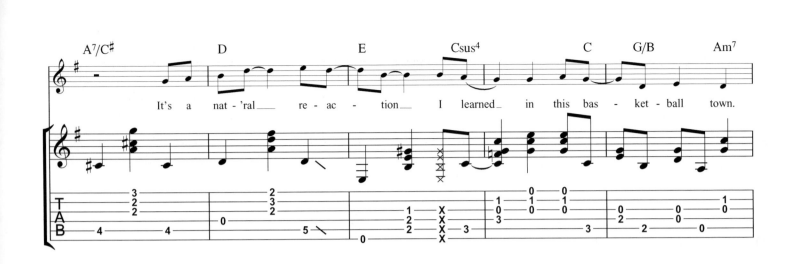

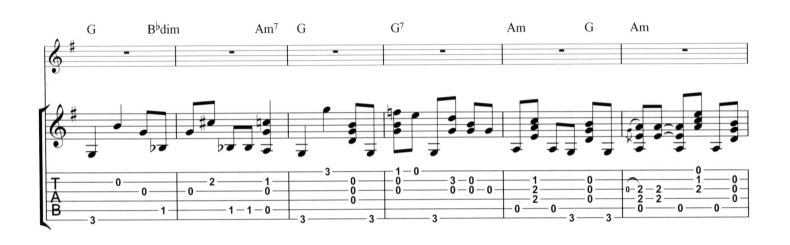

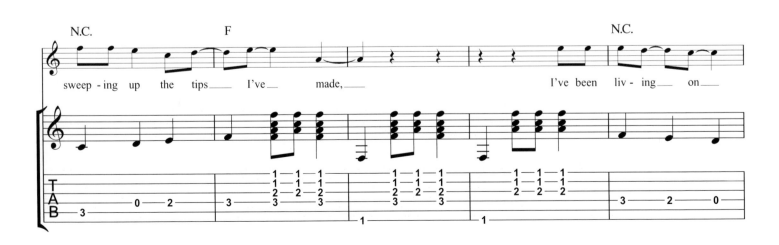

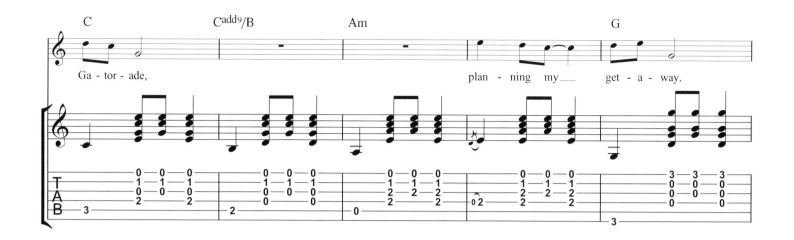

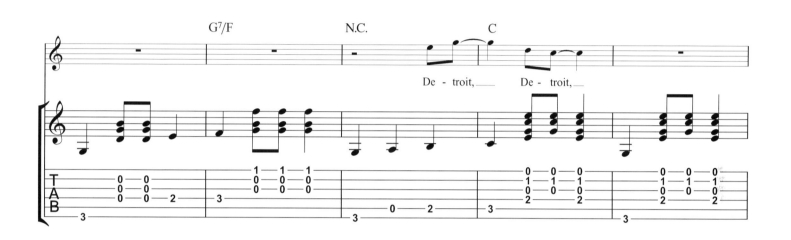

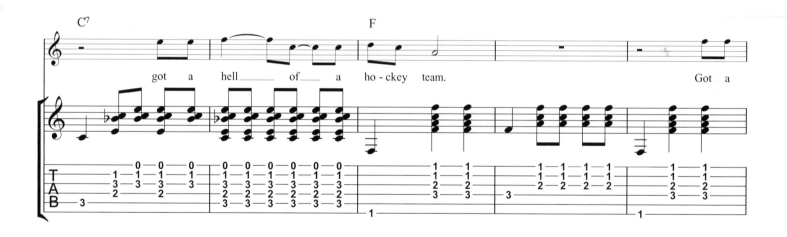

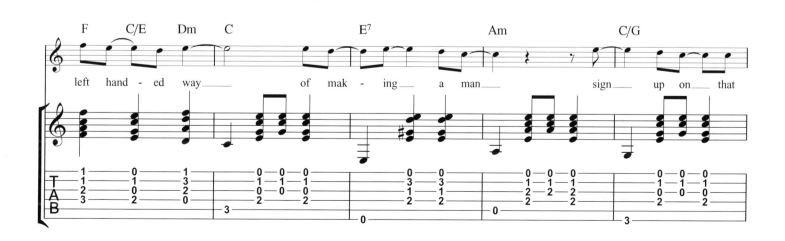

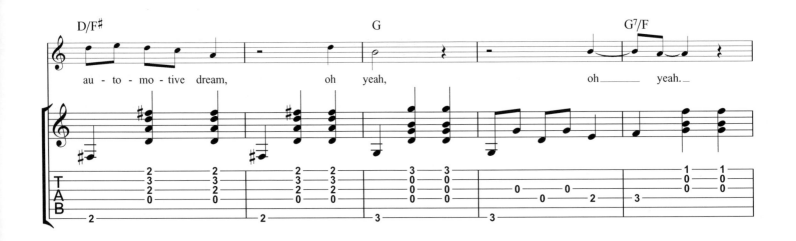

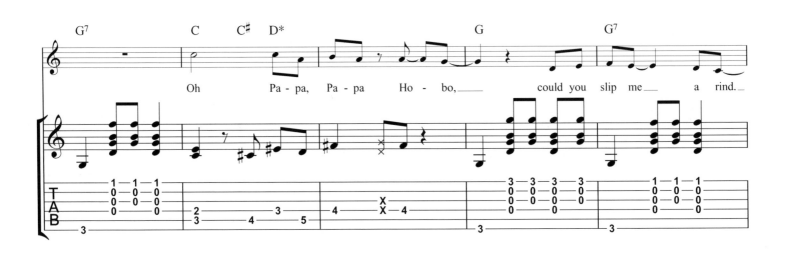

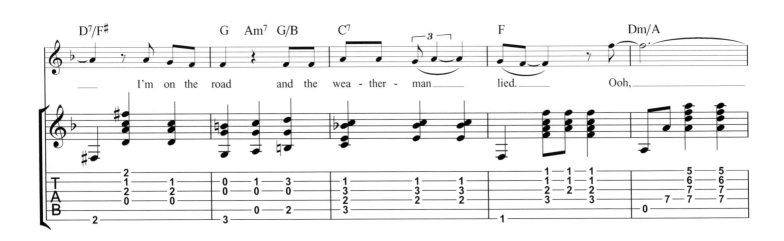

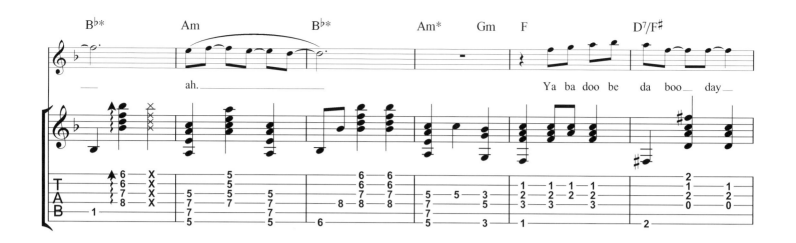

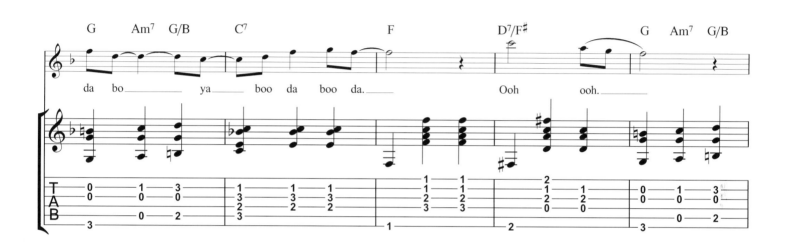

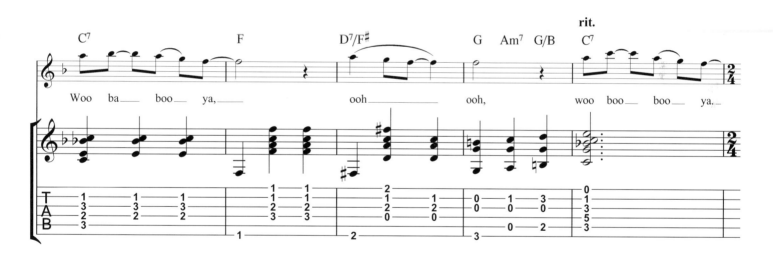

RUN THAT BODY DOWN

WORDS & MUSIC BY PAUL SIMON

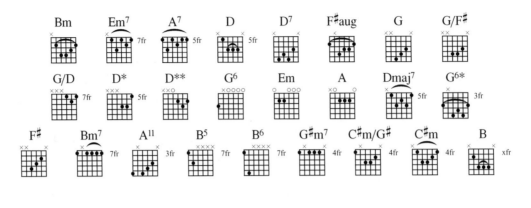

1. Went to my doc - tor yes - ter - day.
2. I came back home and I_____ went to bed,

Ah._____
I_____ was rest - ing my head._____

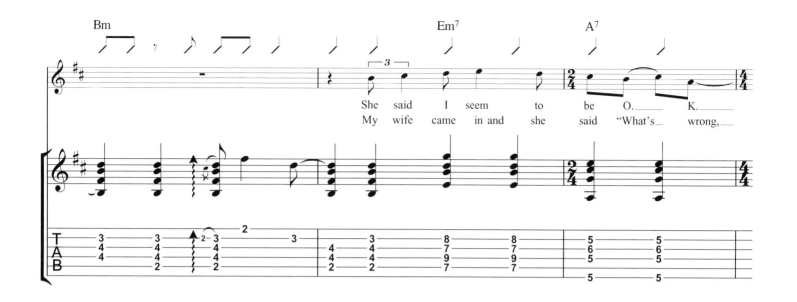

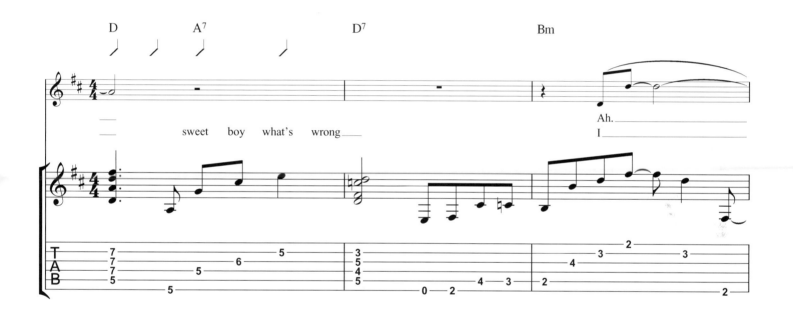

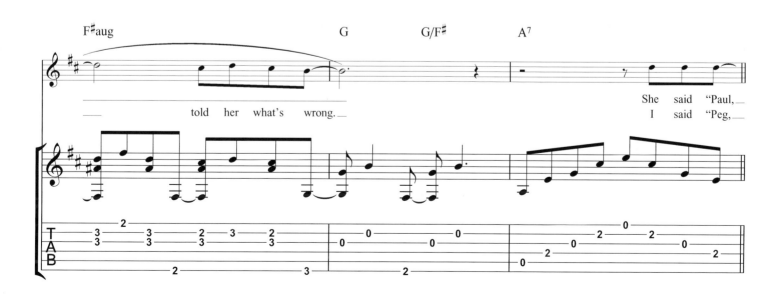

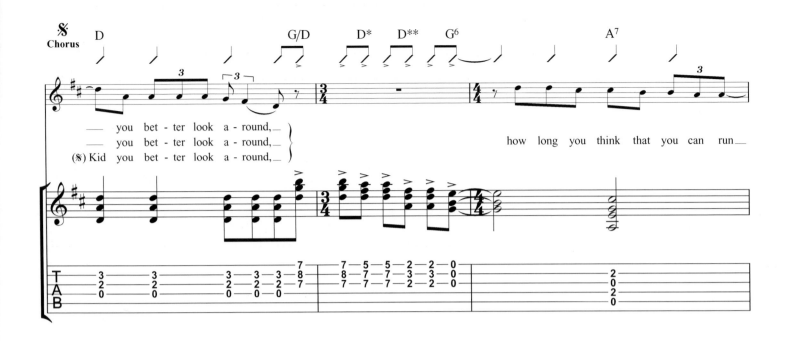

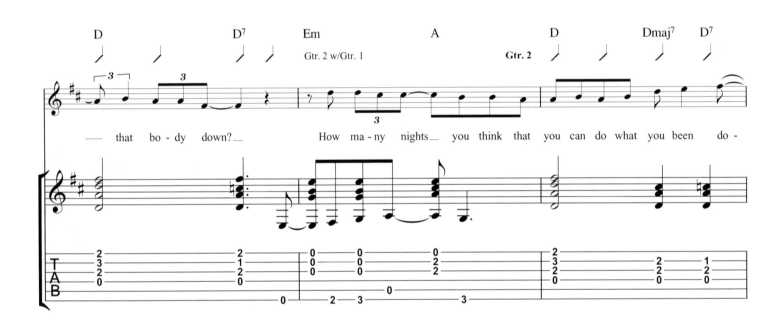

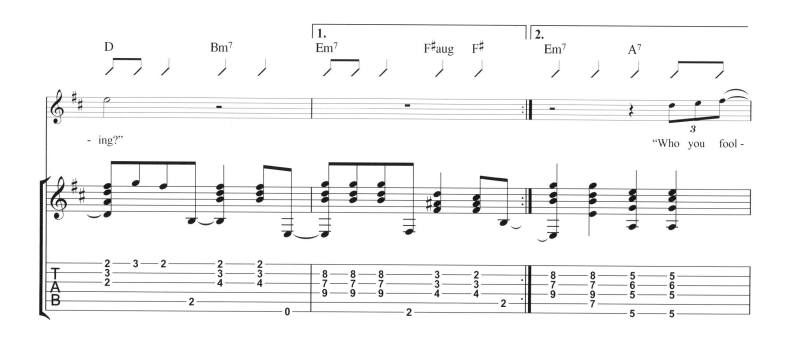

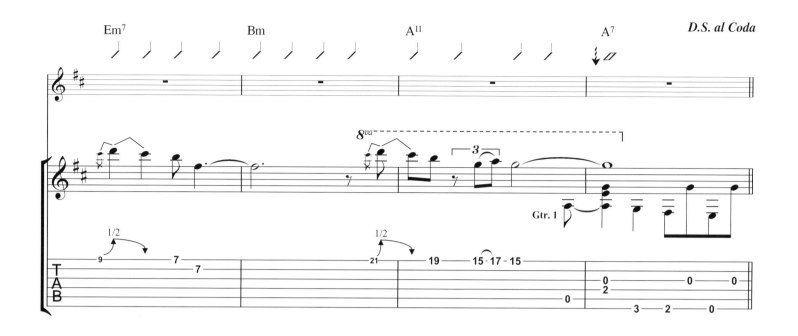

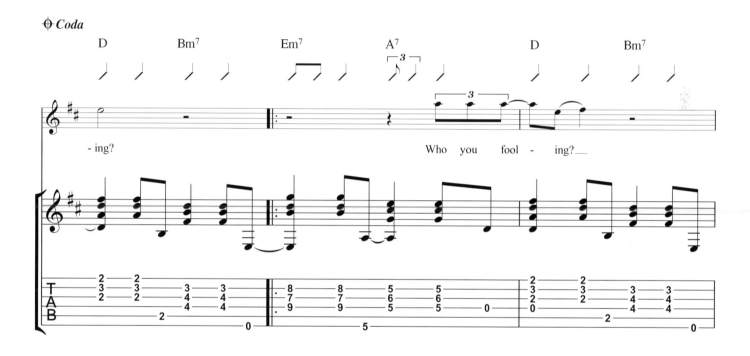

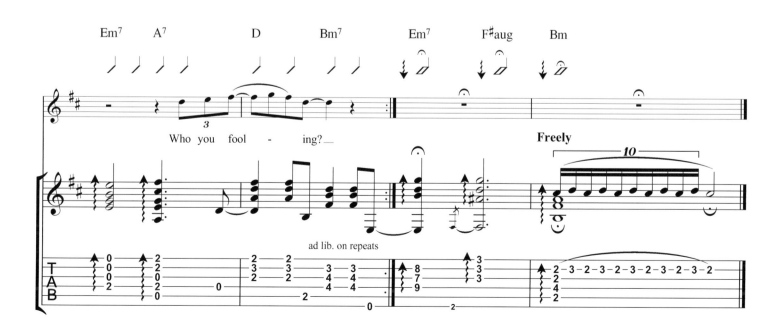

SOMETHING SO RIGHT

WORDS & MUSIC BY PAUL SIMON

Capo 1st Fret

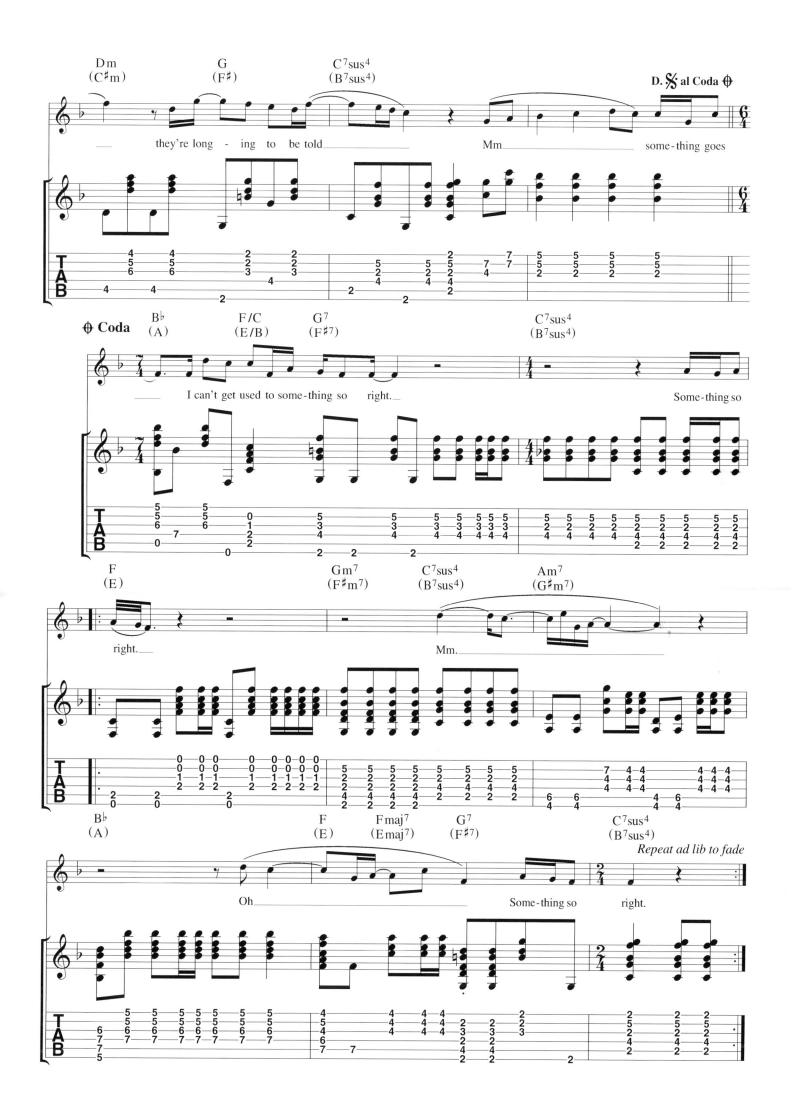

ST. JUDY'S COMET

WORDS & MUSIC BY PAUL SIMON

Won't you run, come see Saint Ju - dy's Co - met roll__

__ a - cross the skies,__ and leave a spray__ of dia - monds in its wake.__

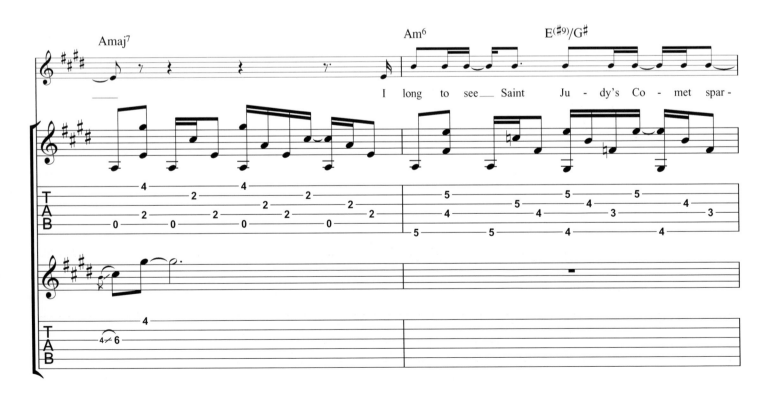

Amaj⁷

Am⁶

E⁽♯⁹⁾/G♯

__ I long to see__ Saint Ju - dy's Co - met spar -

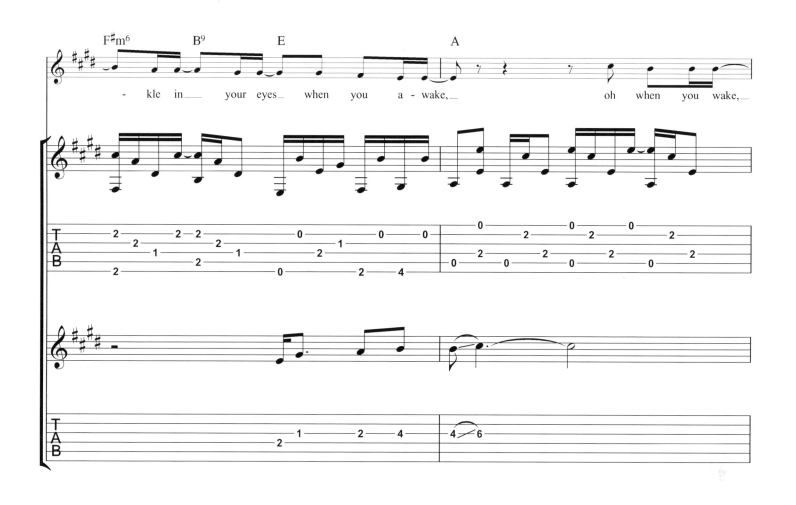

- kle in___ your eyes___ when you a - wake,___ oh when you wake,___

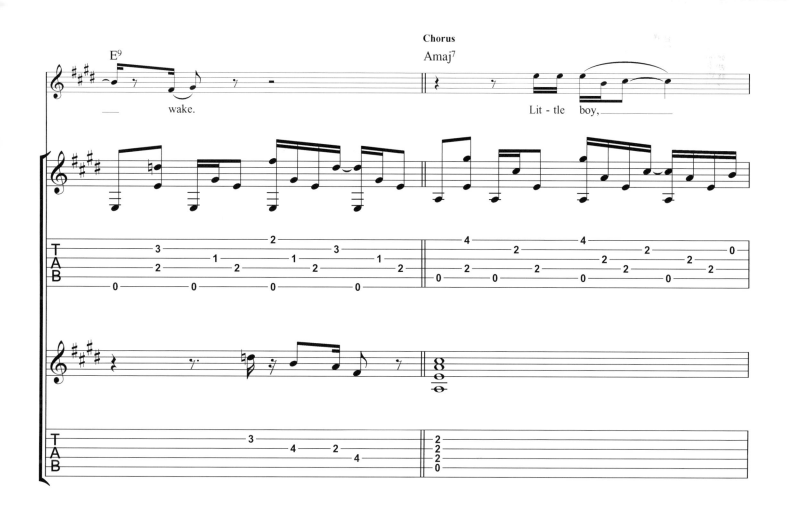

___ wake.

Chorus

Lit - tle boy,___

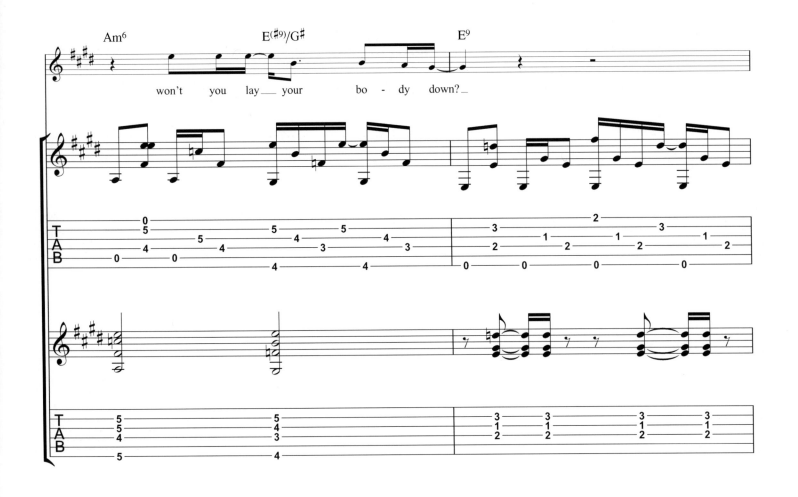

won't you lay___ your bo - dy down?___

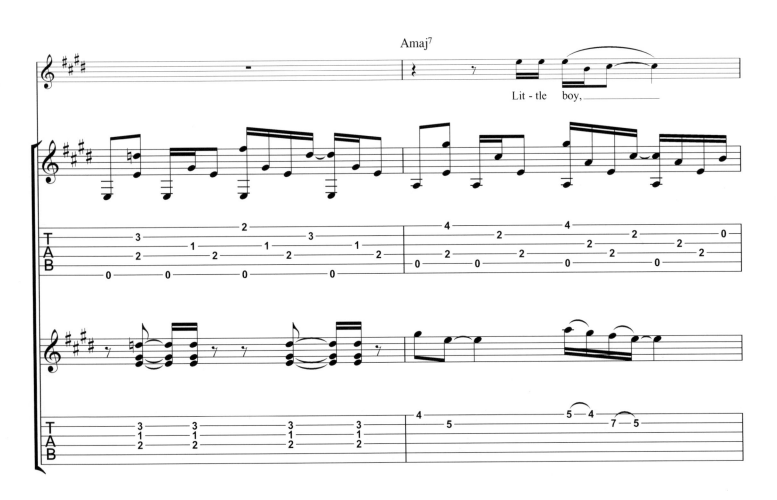

Lit - tle boy,___

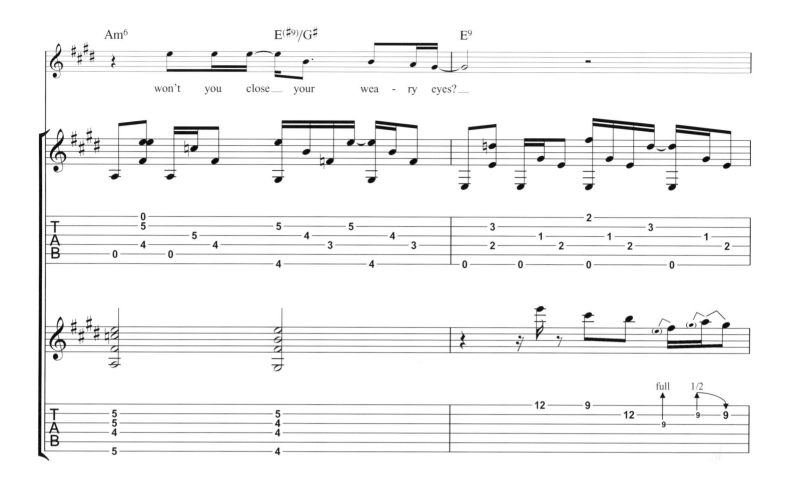

won't you close your wea-ry eyes?

Ain't no-thing flash-ing but the fire-flies.

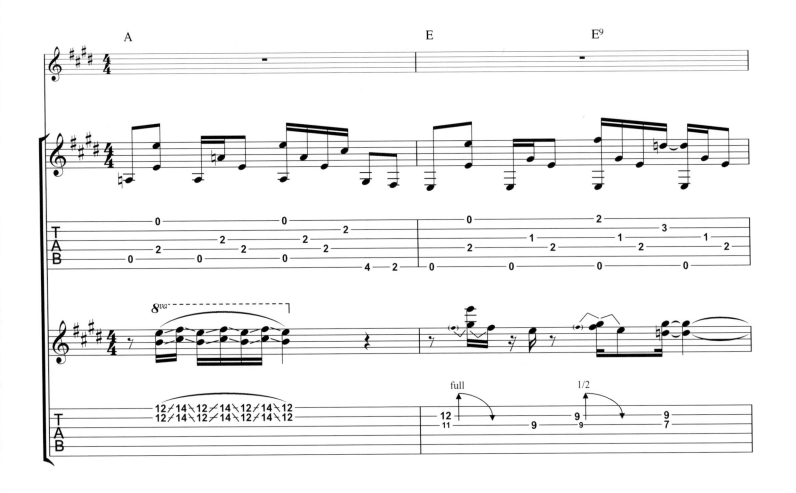

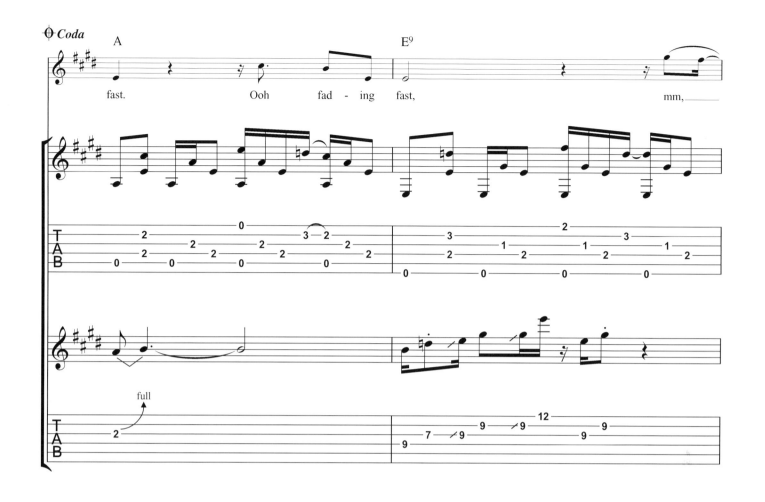

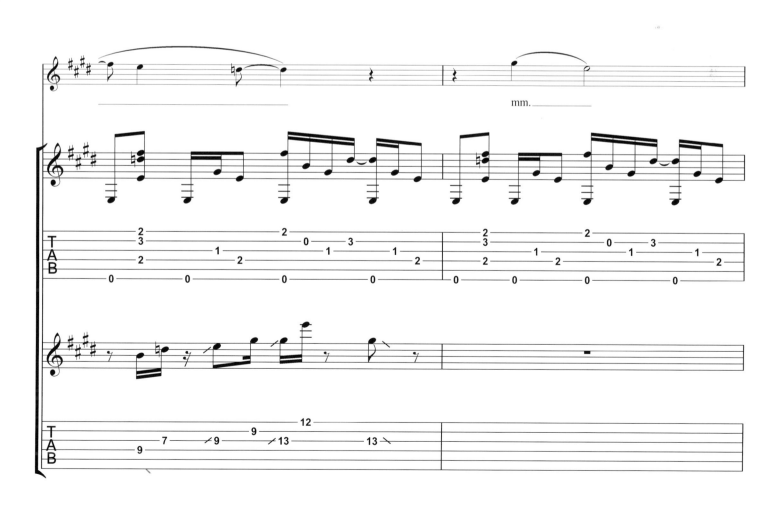

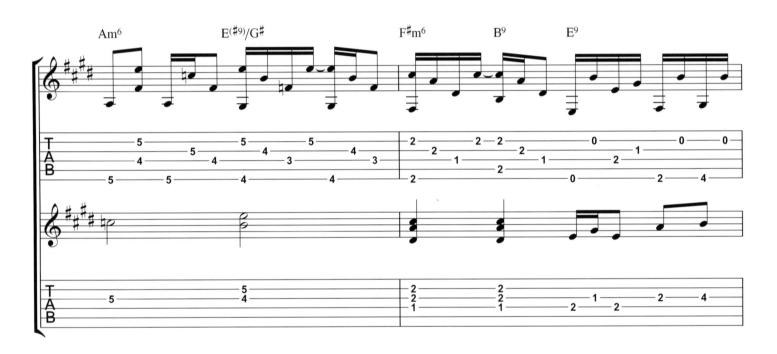

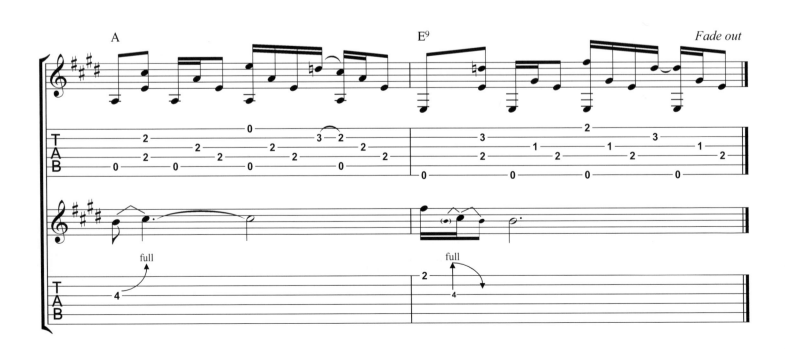

PEACE LIKE A RIVER

WORDS & MUSIC BY PAUL SIMON

Solo

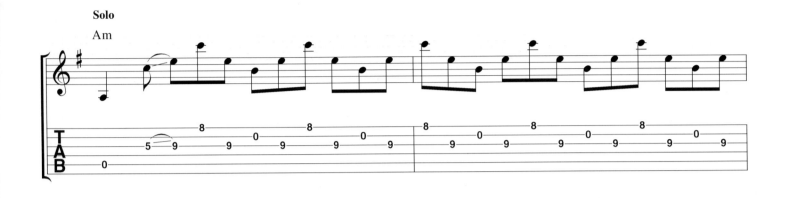

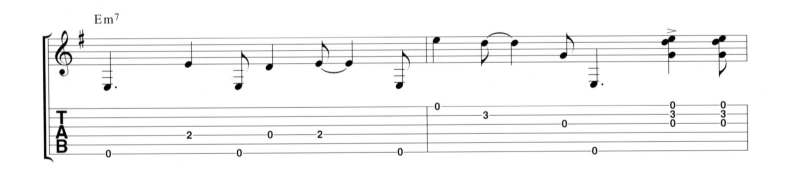

D. % al Coda ⊕

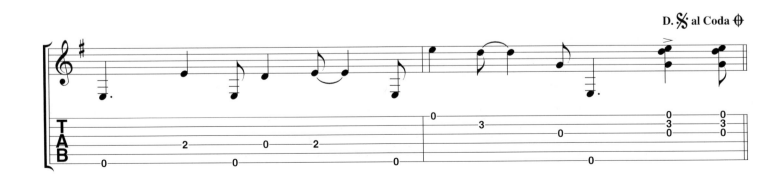

116

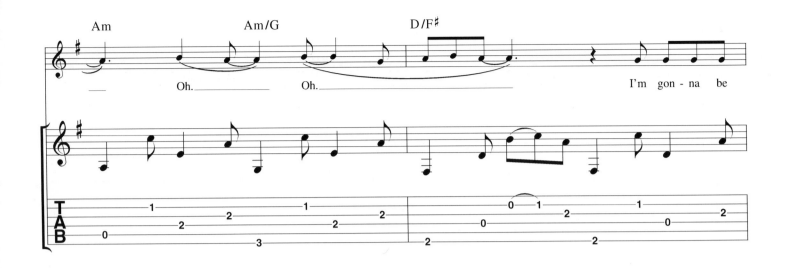

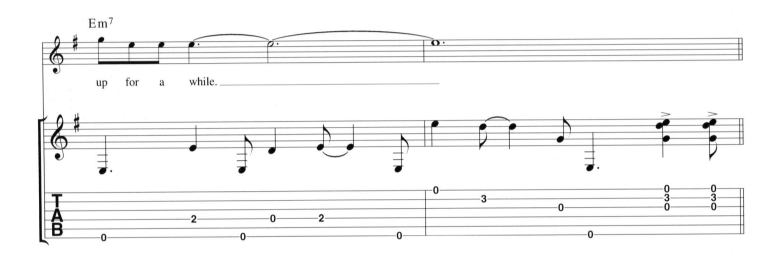

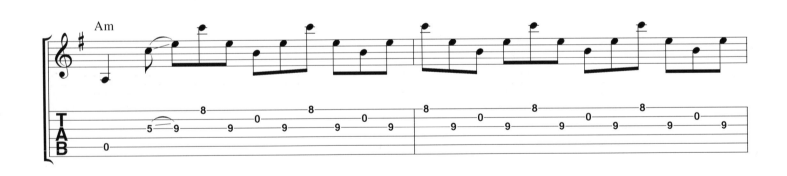

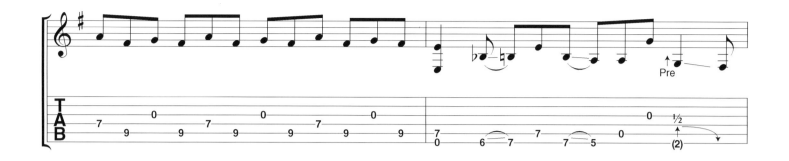

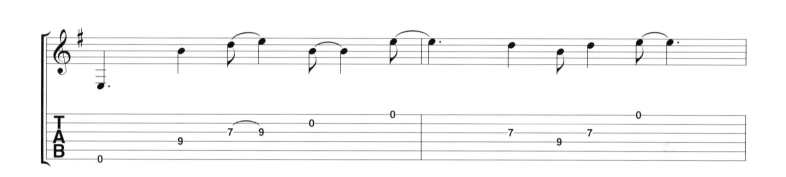

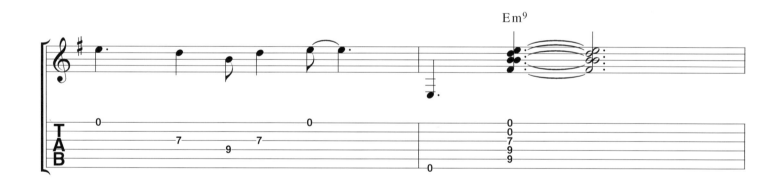

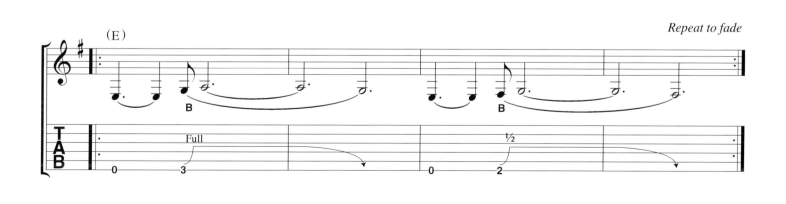

TAKE ME TO THE MARDI GRAS

WORDS & MUSIC BY PAUL SIMON

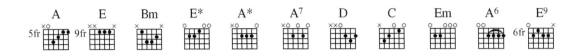

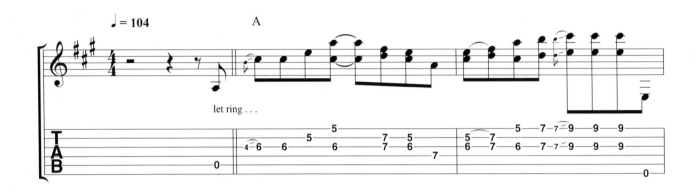

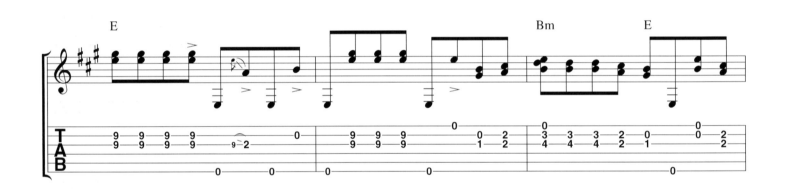

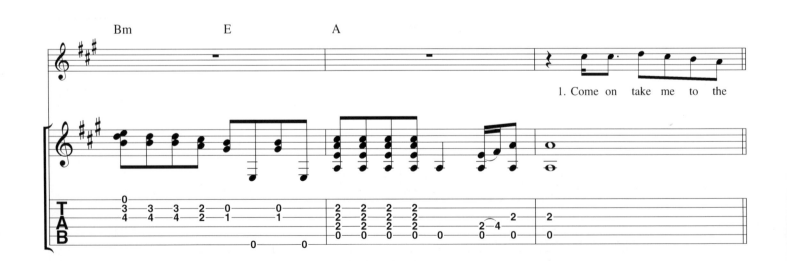

1. Come on take me to the

Toom - ba toom - ba toom - ba Mar - di Gras

toom - ba toom - ba toom - ba

day.

Hey___ hey_____ hey___

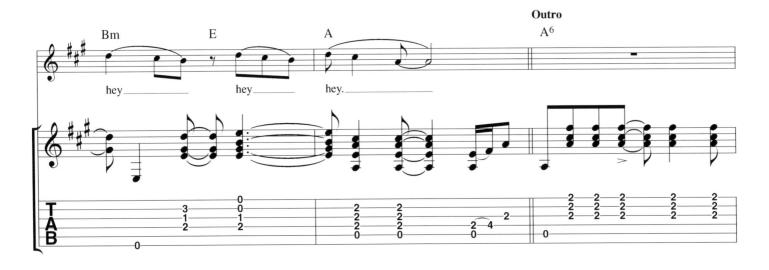

hey___ hey___ hey.

Outro

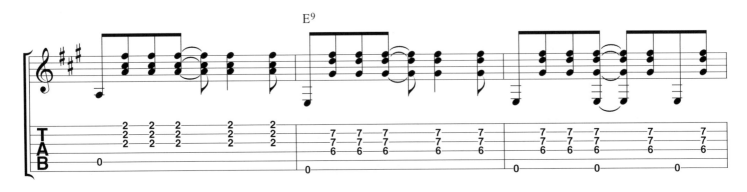

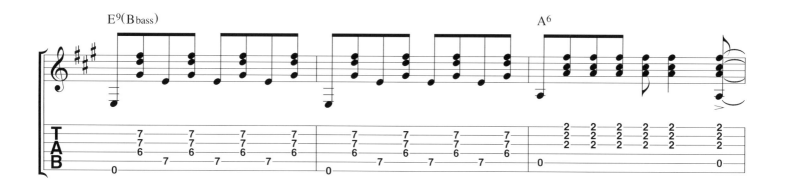

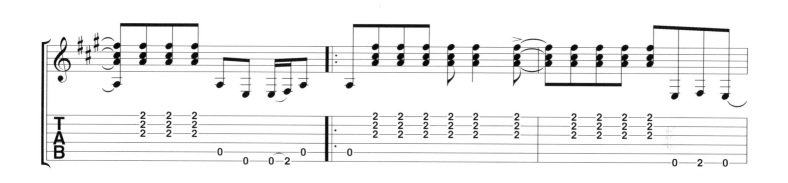

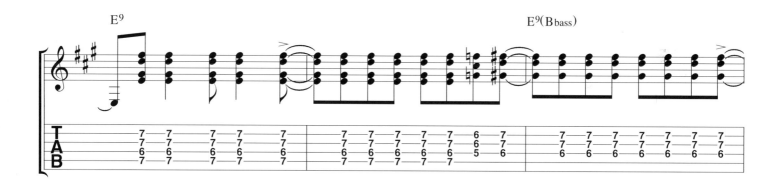

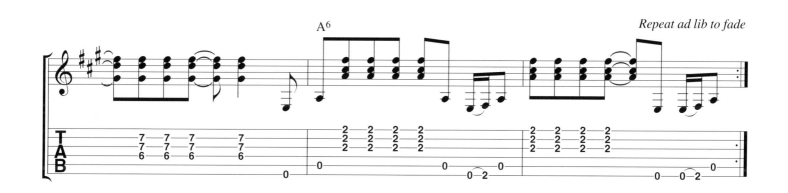

GUITAR TABLATURE EXPLAINED

Guitar music can be notated in three different ways: on a musical stave, in tablature, and in rhythm slashes.

RHYTHM SLASHES are written above the stave. Strum chords in the rhythm indicated. Round noteheads indicate single notes.

THE MUSICAL STAVE shows pitches and rhythms and is divided by lines into bars. Pitches are named after the first seven letters of the alphabet.

TABLATURE graphically represents the guitar fingerboard. Each horizontal line represents a string, and each number represents a fret.

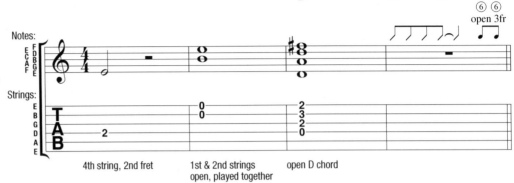

4th string, 2nd fret
1st & 2nd strings open, played together
open D chord

DEFINITIONS FOR SPECIAL GUITAR NOTATION

SEMI-TONE BEND: Strike the note and bend up a semi-tone (1/2 step).

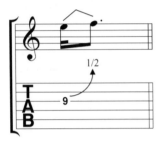

WHOLE-TONE BEND: Strike the note and bend up a whole-tone (whole step).

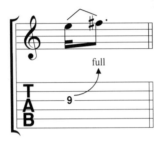

GRACE NOTE BEND: Strike the note and bend as indicated. Play the first note as quickly as possible.

QUARTER-TONE BEND: Strike the note and bend up a 1/4 step.

BEND & RELEASE: Strike the note and bend up as indicated, then release back to the original note.

COMPOUND BEND & RELEASE: Strike the note and bend up and down in the rhythm indicated.

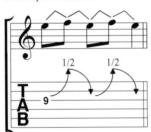

PRE-BEND: Bend the note as indicated, then strike it.

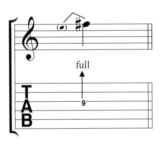

PRE-BEND & RELEASE: Bend the note as indicated. Strike it and release the note back to the original pitch.

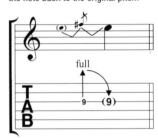

UNISON BEND: Strike the two notes simultaneously and bend the lower note up to the pitch of the higher.

BEND & RESTRIKE: Strike the note and bend as indicated then restrike the string where the symbol occurs.

BEND, HOLD AND RELEASE: Same as bend and release but hold the bend for the duration of the tie.

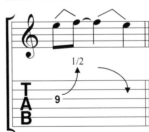

BEND AND TAP: Bend the note as indicated and tap the higher fret while still holding the bend.

VIBRATO: The string is vibrated by rapidly bending and releasing the note with the fretting hand.

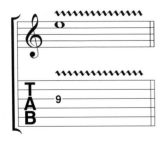

HAMMER-ON: Strike the first note with one finger, then sound the second note (on the same string) with another finger by fretting it without picking.

PULL-OFF: Place both fingers on the notes to be sounded, strike the first note and without picking, pull the finger off to sound the second note.

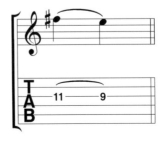

LEGATO SLIDE (GLISS): Strike the first note and then slide the same fret-hand finger up or down to the second note. The second note is not struck.

SHIFT SLIDE (GLISS & RESTRIKE): Same as legato slide, except the second note is struck.

TRILL: Very rapidly alternate between the notes indicated by continuously hammering on and pulling off.

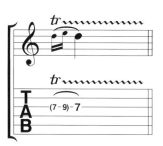

TAPPING: Hammer ("tap") the fret indicated with the pick-hand index or middle finger and pull off to the note fretted by the fret hand.

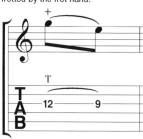

PICK SCRAPE: The edge of the pick is rubbed down (or up) the string, producing a scratchy sound.

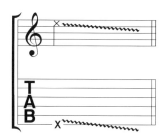

MUFFLED STRINGS: A percussive sound is produced by laying the fret hand across the string(s) without depressing, and striking them with the pick hand.

NATURAL HARMONIC: Strike the note while the fret-hand lightly touches the string directly over the fret indicated.

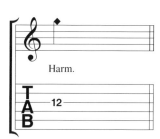

PINCH HARMONIC: The note is fretted normally and a harmonic is produced by adding the edge of the thumb or the tip of the index finger of the pick hand to the normal pick attack.

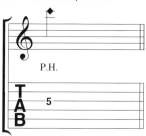

HARP HARMONIC: The note is fretted normally and a harmonic is produced by gently resting the pick hand's index finger directly above the indicated fret (in brackets) while plucking the appropriate string.

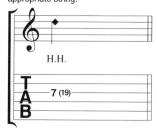

PALM MUTING: The note is partially muted by the pick hand lightly touching the string(s) just before the bridge.

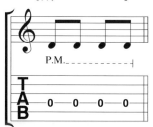

RAKE: Drag the pick across the strings indicated with a single motion.

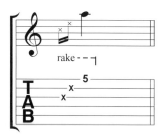

TREMOLO PICKING: The note is picked as rapidly and continuously as possible.

ARPEGGIATE: Play the notes of the chord indicated by quickly rolling them from bottom to top.

SWEEP PICKING: Rhythmic downstroke and/or upstroke motion across the strings.

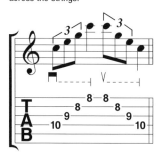

VIBRATO DIVE BAR AND RETURN: The pitch of the note or chord is dropped a specific number of steps (in rhythm) then returned to the original pitch.

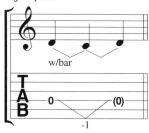

VIBRATO BAR SCOOP: Depress the bar just before striking the note, then quickly release the bar.

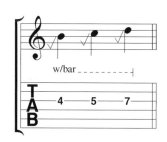

VIBRATO BAR DIP: Strike the note and then immediately drop a specific number of steps, then release back to the original pitch.

ADDITIONAL MUSICAL DEFINITIONS

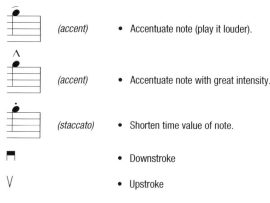

- (accent)   • Accentuate note (play it louder).

- (accent)   • Accentuate note with great intensity.

- (staccato)   • Shorten time value of note.

- ■   • Downstroke

- V   • Upstroke

NOTE: Tablature numbers in brackets mean:
1. The note is sustained, but a new articulation (such as hammer on or slide) begins.
2. A note may be fretted but not necessarily played.

D.%. al Coda

D.C. al Fine

tacet

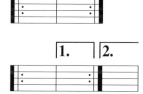

- Go back to the sign (%), then play until the bar marked **To Coda** ⊕ then skip to the section marked ⊕ **Coda**.

- Go back to the beginning of the song and play until the bar marked **Fine**.

- Instrument is silent (drops out).

- Repeat bars between signs.

- When a repeated section has different endings, play the first ending only the first time and the second ending only the second time.

Wise Publications
14/15 Berners Street, London W1T 3LJ, England.

Exclusive Distributors:
Music Sales Limited
Distribution Centre, Newmarket Road, Bury St. Edmunds, Suffolk IP33 3YB, England.
Music Sales Corporation
257 Park Avenue South, New York, NY10010, United States of America.
Music Sales Pty Limited
20 Resolution Drive, Caringbah, NSW 2229, Australia.

Order No. PS11572
ISBN 1-84449-181-1
This book © Copyright 2003 by Wise Publications.

Cover designed by Fresh Lemon.
Music arranged by Matt Cowe and Martin Shellard.
Music processed by Paul Ewers Music Design.
Compiled by Nick Crispin.
Printed in Great Britain.

Your Guarantee of Quality
As publishers, we strive to produce every book to the highest commercial standards.
The music has been freshly engraved and the book has been carefully designed to
minimise awkward page turns and to make playing from it a real pleasure.
Particular care has been given to specifying acid-free, neutral-sized paper made from pulps
which have not been elemental chlorine bleached.
This pulp is from farmed sustainable forests and was produced with special regard for the environment.
Throughout, the printing and binding have been planned to ensure a sturdy, attractive
publication which should give years of enjoyment.
If your copy fails to meet our high standards, please inform us and we will gladly replace it.

Also available
Acoustic Masters for Guitar: Cat Stevens
Seventeen great acoustic guitar tracks (Order No. AM91350)

Acoustic Masters for Guitar: David Gray
Eightteen superb acoustic guitar tracks (Order No. AM944340)

www.musicsales.com